THE MOSELLE CYCLE ROUTE

FROM THE SOURCE TO THE RHINE AT KOBLENZ

About the Author

Mike Wells has been a keen cyclist for over 20 years. Starting with UK Sustrans routes, like Lon Las Cymru in Wales and the C2C route across northern England, he soon moved on to long-distance routes in continental Europe and beyond. These include cycling both the Camino and Ruta de la Plata to Santiago de la Compostela, a traverse of Cuba from end to end, a circumnavigation of Iceland and a trip across Lapland to the North Cape.

This is Mike's second cycling guide for Cicerone, following his guide to cycling the Rhine from source to sea. Indeed, it was while preparing the Rhine cycle guide that he became aware of the well-developed cycling infrastructure along the nearby Moselle. The two books could be used together to create an attractive circular route starting in Basel, Mulhouse or Koblenz then cycling down one river and back up the other.

Other Cicerone guides by the author
The Adlerweg
The Rhine Cycle Route

THE MOSELLE CYCLE ROUTE

FROM THE SOURCE TO THE RHINE AT KOBLENZ
by Mike Wells

2 POLICE SQUARE, MILNTHORPE, CUMBRIA LA7 7PY
www.cicerone.co.uk

© Mike Wells 2014
First edition 2014
ISBN: 978 1 85284 721 0

Printed in China on behalf of Latitude Press Ltd

Route mapping by Lovell Johns www.lovelljohns.com
Contains OpenStreetMap.org data © OpenStreetMap
contributors, CC-BY-SA. NASA relief data courtesy of ESRI.

*To my grandchildren Atlanta and Alexander, who have just been given
their first bicycles, in the hope that they may have many adventurous
cycle rides when they grow older.*

Advice to Readers

While every effort is made by our authors to ensure the accuracy of
guidebooks as they go to print, changes can occur during the lifetime of an
edition. If we know of any, there will be an Updates tab on this book's page
on the Cicerone website (www.cicerone.co.uk), so please check before
planning your trip. We also advise that you check information about such
things as transport, accommodation and shops locally. Even rights of way
can be altered over time. We are always grateful for information about
any discrepancies between a guidebook and the facts on the ground, sent
by email to info@cicerone.co.uk or by post to Cicerone, 2 Police Square,
Milnthorpe LA7 7PY, United Kingdom.

Front cover: Cycling through vineyards between Trittenheim and Neumagen
(Stage 11)

CONTENTS

THE MOSELLE CYCLE ROUTE

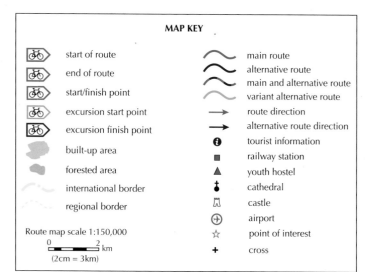

MAP KEY

🚲	start of route	〰	main route
🚲	end of route	〰	alternative route
🚲	start/finish point	〰	main and alternative route
🚲	excursion start point	〰	variant alternative route
🚲	excursion finish point	→	route direction
	built-up area	→	alternative route direction
	forested area	🛈	tourist information
	international border	◼	railway station
	regional border	▲	youth hostel
		🛉	cathedral
Route map scale 1:150,000		🏰	castle
0 — 2 km		⊕	airport
(2cm = 3km)		☆	point of interest
		✛	cross

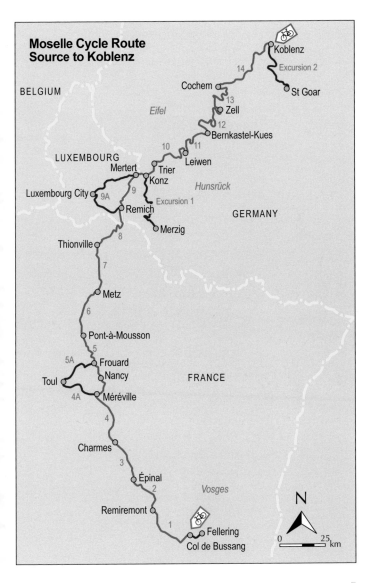

Moselle Cycle Route
Source to Koblenz

The vineyards of the Calmont slope rise behind Bremm (Stage 13)

INTRODUCTION

The cycle route follows the Canal des Vosges through Lorraine (Stage 3)

To many people the greatest thing about the Moselle is not the water that flows in the river: rather it is the wine that is produced along its banks. And what great wine it is. The Riesling grape grows at its very best on the slatey slopes of the Moselle gorge and the best of the resulting wines, from famous villages like Bernkastel and Piesport, are among Germany's finest. But for the cyclist, the Moselle offers much more than either wine or water.

Rising in the Vosges Mountains in eastern France, the Moselle flows generally north through the French region of Lorraine and the German *Land* (state) of Rheinland-Pfalz. Once in Germany it follows a deep meandering gorge between the Hunsrück and Eifel Mountains before joining the Rhine at Deutsches Eck ('German corner') in Koblenz.

The great attraction to a cyclist of following a river from its source is that, once you have reached the start, it's all downhill. From the easily reached source near the Col de Bussang, the Moselle cycle route descends over 650m to the Rhine at Koblenz, 512km distant. The cycling is straightforward, with much of the route following well-surfaced cycle tracks, often along the riverbank or canal towpaths. On those occasions where roads are used, these are usually quiet country routes. All three of the countries passed through – France, Luxembourg and Germany – are highly cycle-friendly, and motorists will generally give you plenty of room. This route is suitable both for experienced long-distance cyclists, and for those who have not done much cycle touring and wish to start with a straightforward, easily followed route.

The route mostly follows French and German national cycle trails, with a high standard of waymarking for most of the journey. This guide breaks the route into 14 stages, averaging just over 36km per stage. A fit cyclist, covering two stages per day, should be able to complete the trip in a week. In addition, there are two variants and two excursions that visit attractive locations just off the main route. Allowing two weeks would enable these to be included, provide more time for sightseeing and allow the route to be cycled at a leisurely pace. You can break the journey at almost any point, as there are many places to stay along the way. These are suitable for all budgets, varying from 13 Hostelling International youth hostels through B&Bs, guesthouses and hotels. If you don't mind the extra weight of camping gear, there are many official campsites.

The Moselle offers variety: from the delights of French cuisine to the pleasures of German Riesling; from rolling foothills and wide valleys in Lorraine to the narrow meandering gorge in Rheinland-Pfalz; from great historic cities like Nancy, Metz and Trier to pretty villages on the Boucles de la Moselle and spread out along the gorge; from Roman fortifications to 20th-century defence lines; and from two of Europe's largest countries to Luxembourg, one of its smallest.

The sheer beauty of the route running through the narrow Moselle gorge between Trier and Cochem is rightly regarded as one of Europe's great tourist attractions, evidenced by the large number of cyclists you will find along this section. Fortunately there is infrastructure, in the form of accommodation, restaurants, campsites and asphalt cycle tracks, to cope with it. The rest of the river is much less well-known, although no less attractive to the cycle tourist. Apart from two easily bypassed sections of rough canal towpath north and south of Nancy and a quiet country road between Remiremont and Épinal, asphalt cycle tracks have been provided along almost the whole route. While there are fewer places to stay overnight before the route reaches Trier, demand is consequently smaller and no problems should be found obtaining accommodation, food and beverages.

Huge quantities of wine are produced along the German part of the Moselle gorge, but this is not the only beverage you will find along the way. Quality wine is also produced around Toul on the Boucles de la Moselle and the Luxembourg side of the gorge is a large producer, particularly famous for its Crémant sparkling wine. Lorraine

The steepest part of the Moselle Gorge between Brem and Eller (Stage 13)

has a growing number of local micro-breweries, producing a wide variety of styles of beer. In Lorraine too, golden Mirabelle plums are used to make fruit schnapps and in the Saar valley *viez*, a local form of cider, is produced. Be sure to sample these local beverages, but do so in the evening: cycling and alcohol do not mix!

BACKGROUND

Geographically, the Moselle has three distinct sections:

- *Haute-Moselle* (Upper Moselle, Stages 1–4) is the non-navigable part of the river running through the limestone Vosges foothills from the source to Neuves-Maisons, south of Nancy. Below Épinal, the river is followed by the Canal des Vosges.

- *Moselle canalisée* (Middle Moselle, Stages 5–8) is the navigable, partly straightened section through a broad, partly industrialised valley from Nancy to the Franco–German–Luxembourg border.

- *Moseltal* (Moselle Gorge, Stages 9–14) is the lower part of the river where it has cut a tight, meandering gorge between the Hunsrück and Eifel Mountains. This is the section famous for the production of Mosel wine.

Nowadays the point where the Moselle reaches the Hunsrück is the national border between the French region of Lorraine, the German state of Rheinland-Pfalz and the small independent Duchy of Luxembourg. But historically, political control has

11

seldom replicated geography. Indeed the history of the Moselle basin for the past 500 years has been of control passing back and forward between two often bellicose nations.

The Holy Roman Empire

In medieval times Lorraine, Trier and Luxembourg were three semi-independent states and members of the mainly Germanic Holy Roman Empire (HRE), along with a plethora of other small independent states across what is now Germany. These states each had their own government structures led by a ruler with a title such as prince, duke, *margrave* ('marquis') or, in some places – like Trier – bishop. The titular leader of the HRE was the Holy Roman Emperor. When it became necessary to appoint a new emperor, these various rulers would gather together in conclave and elect one of their number as emperor. As a result they became known jointly as Electors, an early, although very limited, form of democracy. Over time the larger, stronger states came to dominate these arrangements and the Habsburg rulers of Austria more or less assumed the title of Holy Roman Emperor, while at the same time the central unifying influence and power of the HRE declined.

Growth of French influence

To the west of the HRE was France, a country that grew steadily, first by ejecting the English from their territories in continental Europe and then by assimilating other smaller states. As France spread east so it started to come into conflict with the Empire. The first parts of Lorraine (the three

Trier's Porta Nigra Roman gate (Stage 9)

bishoprics of Metz, Toul and Verdun) were annexed in 1552 but the main turning point came during the Thirty Years' War (1618–1648). While this was in essence a religious struggle for power between catholic and protestant elements within the HRE, many neighbouring states, including France, were drawn into the conflict. In 1641 the French captured the whole of Lorraine, only to withdraw again in 1648 under the terms of the Treaty of Westphalia, which ended the war. This treaty also confirmed French rule over the three bishoprics, which then became the French province of les Trois-Évêchés.

The French returned in 1670, during the reign of Louis XIV, this time going on to invade Trier and the Rhineland too. They withdrew again in 1697. During this period of French control the Duke of Lorraine, Charles V, sought refuge in Austria, where his son Leopold was brought up in the Habsburg court. Return to full independence was short-lived. In 1736, at the end of the war of the Polish Succession, Francis Stephen, who had succeeded his father Leopold as Duke, was deposed and replaced by a French-nominated successor. This was Stanislas, former king of Poland, whose daughter was married to Louis XV, and who commissioned the beautiful palaces and squares that make up the centre of Nancy. Incidentally, Francis Stephen did not do too badly out of this arrangement: created Duke of Tuscany by the Habsburgs, he went on to marry Maria Theresa, become

Archduke of Austria and Holy Roman Emperor! During Stanislas's rule, French influence over Lorraine steadily grew and, on his death in 1766, control passed directly to the French crown. Shortly after, during the French Revolutionary Wars (1789–1799), Lorraine was reorganised into four French *départements* (counties) of Moselle (north), Meurthe (centre), Meuse (west) and Vosges (south).

During the reign of the Emperor Napoleon, French power reached its zenith. A series of military campaigns saw the French gain control of much of western and central Europe. Trier and the Rhineland were integrated into France, with towns such as Koblenz and Mainz assuming French names (Coblence and Mayence respectively). In Trier the electoral bishopric was abolished after 900 years. By sweeping away the multiplicity of small states that formed the HRE, Napoleon effectively ended the Empire. When he was defeated in 1815 by the combined forces of Britain and Prussia, the latter was one of two German states that emerged in a strong position (the other was Bavaria). These two states stepped into the void created by the end of the HRE, with the Prussians taking control of much of northern Germany including Trier and the northern Rhineland.

The Prussians arrive

Despite a final rally to arms in 1840, when France threatened to invade the Rhineland, this was the end of

13

The equestrian statue of Kaiser Wilhelm I at Deutsches Eck in Koblenz (Stage 14)

France as the expansionary aggressor. Power now turned steadily to the east. By 1870 the Prussians, led by the 'Iron Chancellor' Bismarck, had succeeded in unifying Germany, and during the Franco–Prussian War (1870–1871) they captured much of eastern France and threatened Paris. The treaty that ended this war gave the west bank of the Rhine (Alsace) and the Moselle département of Lorraine (including the industrial cities of Metz and Thionville) to a newly established German Empire. French refugees from these areas arrived in the rest of Lorraine, giving a stimulus to the growth of industry, particularly textiles, in towns like Épinal along the Moselle.

German occupation lasted nearly 50 years. During this period the French language was supressed and a process of Germanisation carried out (as a legacy of this time, the trains in Alsace and northern Lorraine run on the right, compared with on the left in the rest of France). German control lasted until 1919, when the treaty of Versailles, which ended the First World War (1914–1918), returned Alsace and the Moselle département to France, ordered German military withdrawal from the Rhineland and created a small buffer state (Saarland) between France and Germany. Under French rule (1919–1940) a reverse process occurred, with the German language banned. In 1935 Germany, now under Nazi control, reoccupied the Rhineland and Saarland. A brief period of draconian German occupation of France (1940–1944)

14

occurred during the Second World War, followed by a final return to French rule after the defeat of Nazi Germany. There were families whose sons fought for Germany in 1914–1918, then began the Second World War fighting for France, only to be re-conscripted into the German army in 1940, most probably fighting and dying on the eastern front.

All these years of conflict have left the region peppered with military hardware, from Roman fortifications, through medieval castles and fortified military towns to integrated defensive lines and concrete anti-tank defences, each passing into history as the technological progress of warfare made them redundant. The great French fort builders Vauban (1633–1707), Séré de Rivières (1815–1895)

and Maginot (1877–1932) all left their mark. Riverside settlements still show the scars of battle, particularly from the Second World War, where intensive bombing was followed by destructive land warfare and fierce fighting as Allied forces tried to cross the river. This is evident especially in the bridges, which were almost all destroyed during 1944–1945 and have been subsequently rebuilt.

Luxembourg

Throughout this period, Luxembourg too has suffered at the hands of its French and German neighbours. Having been an important member of the HRE (three of its 14th and 15th-century dukes became Holy Roman Emperor) it lost its independence in 1437 when power passed

Sentry duty outside Luxembourg Grand Ducal Palace (Stage 9A)

The birthplace of Karl Marx in Trier, now a museum (Stage 9)

to the Burgundians. Over the following centuries control alternated between Bourbon French, Austrian and Spanish Habsburgs, Napoleonic French, Prussia and the Netherlands, with Luxembourg losing over 75 per cent of its original territory in land grabs by France (1659), Prussia (1815) and Belgium (1839). Since 1815 the country has had a close relationship with the Netherlands, even sharing a joint monarchy until 1890. Despite a policy of neutrality, Luxembourg was invaded by Germany in both the First and Second World Wars.

The modern era

The 500-year history of the Moselle basin being a pawn between French- and German-speaking nations may now finally have ended with the entry of France, Germany and Luxembourg into the European Union (1958), as well as the highly symbolic 1985 Schengen Agreement, a treaty signed on a boat on the Moselle near the village of Schengen, at the point at which the borders of French Lorraine, German Rheinland-Pfalz and the Grand Duchy of Luxembourg meet. This treaty led to the free movement of people across European borders and the removal of border controls between countries. As a result, many of the residents of Thionville in France now work across the old 'border' in Luxembourg or Germany, and the borderlands have been designated as a European cross-border super region called Saarlorlux.

River transport

The river itself has a history independent of the political struggle happening around it. Navigation has been going on since at least Roman times. At Neumagen a stone carving of a Roman wine ship was discovered in the 19th century. This is now in the Landesmuseum in Trier, but a concrete copy stands in Neumagen and a full-size replica wooden Roman galley is moored nearby.

A steady process of improving navigation over the centuries led to the removal of tolls and riverine obstructions, the installation of locks and dams to control water flow and the construction of towpaths. Haulage, which had been initially manual or horse-drawn, gave way in the 20th century to moto-tractors and then motorised barges. A major post-Second World War canalisation programme resulted in the opening of the river to larger vessels (up to 110m long) as far as Metz in 1964, Frouard (for Nancy) in 1972 and Neuves-Maisons, 392km and 28 locks upstream from Koblenz, in 1979. Between Frouard and Toul this led to the closure of a short stretch of the Canal de la Marne au Rhin and redirection of its traffic onto the Moselle. Traffic on the river is mostly bulk cargoes and includes oil products, coal, iron ore, scrap metal, finished steel products and building aggregates. Unlike the neighbouring Rhine navigation, there is only a little conveyance of containerised general cargo. The Saar, which joins the Moselle near Trier, has also been canalised to take large barges and there is much interconnecting traffic. Navigation on the Moselle is regulated by an international control commission.

Above Neuves-Maisons the Canal des Vosges (formerly known as the southern section of the Canal de l'Est), which runs alongside the Moselle, allows narrowboats to progress upstream as far as Épinal and provides a connection via the Saône and Rhone with the Mediterranean. There are long-term plans to upgrade this route to take large barges. The Canal de la Marne au Rhin provides a connection for narrowboats from Toul west to the Paris basin (and ultimately the North Sea) and from Frouard east to the middle Rhine at Strasbourg. These canals have little commercial traffic nowadays and are mostly used by leisure craft.

THE ROUTE

The major part of the route described in this book follows two long-distance cycle tracks, the French Véloroute de la Moselle from Épinal to Schengen, which is part of a much longer north–south route across eastern France called the Véloroute Charles-le-Téméraire; and the German Mosel-Radweg from Schengen to Koblenz. These two tracks differ markedly in their continuity and state of completion.

In France a national network of *véloroutes* (cycle tracks) is under development. These are being built to a national standard that includes the following desirable features, wherever

Cycling through the Michelsberg vineyards opposite Piesport (Stage 11)

possible: that the track is on an asphalt surface; that it spans a width of three metres; and that it is separated from vehicular traffic. While the driving force for this programme is regional government (in this case Lorraine), under the French system of local government the implementation and actual construction is the responsibility of local départements. The Véloroute de la Moselle runs through three different départements, between which the degree of completion of the track varies greatly.

The route starts in Vosges département with a short descent, from the river's source in the Vosges Mountains, along a very quiet mountain pass road. In Bussang the first long section of dedicated cycle path is reached (Stage 1). This is the *voie verte* ('greenway') des Hautes Vosges, constructed to national standards along the trackbed of a disused railway through a valley once filled with silver and copper mines. After the first sizeable town (Remiremont), the route continues (Stage 2) using quiet country roads to reach the département capital Épinal. It is unlikely that this stretch will ever be provided with a separate cycle path, although there are plans to mark cycle lanes along the road. The road, however, is so quiet that this hardly seems necessary. Beyond Épinal, the Véloroute de la Moselle is reached, in the form of a more or less complete cycle path (Stage 3) along the towpath of the Canal des Vosges to a point just past Charmes.

Beyond this point, where Vosges ends and you enter Meurthe et Moselle département, very little progress has been made building the véloroute. It is possible to continue (Stage 4) on rough gravel and dirt tracks along the towpath, and this guide does so wherever practical, but some sections on road are necessary where the towpath is impassable. After Méréville, things improve when the route joins the Boucles de la Moselle, a circular véloroute from Nancy via Neuves-Maisons to Toul and back via Frouard along various canal and river towpaths (this is followed in its entirety by using Stages 4A and 5A). Continuing north from Nancy (Stage 5), once the Boucles is left behind beyond Frouard, the surface deteriorates and it is again necessary to use sections of road until Novéant, where Moselle département is reached.

Once in Moselle, things change permanently for the better. A more or less complete cycle path (Stages 6–8), built to national standards and completed in 2012, runs from Novéant past Metz and through Thionville all the way to the German border at Schengen. Waymarked as Véloroute Charles-le-Téméraire, this mostly follows the river or canal banks, although there are sections away from the river circumnavigating riverside lagoons and industrial developments.

North from Schengen the Moselle leaves France, becoming, for a while, the border between Germany (east of the river) and Luxembourg (west of it). It then turns to run through Germany in a deep, iconic gorge meandering between the Hunsrück and Eifel Mountains. A waymarked cycle route, known in German as the Mosel-Radweg, closely follows the river through the gorge, with sign-posted alternatives on both sides of the river. Apart from a few short sections, usually when passing through nature reserves, the track is wide with an asphalt surface. This guide follows the right bank (east of the river) from Konz, at the confluence of the Saar, to Neef before Cochem (Stages 10–13), then switches to the left (west) bank (Stages 13–14) to reach Koblenz, where the Moselle joins the Rhine. While this is the route described in detail, in practice you can cycle on either bank, as there is little to choose between them. The stretch through the gorge is characterised by steep slatey slopes, covered in either vines on the sunnier slopes or forest on the inhospitable north-facing side of the valley.

In addition to the main route, variants are given using the Boucles de la Moselle to visit Toul (see above) and via the small country of Luxembourg (Stage 9A) using mostly dedicated asphalt cycle tracks for a circular tour, visiting the capital. Further excursions, up the Saar valley to Merzig (Excursion 1) and through the Rhine gorge to St Goar (Excursion 2), use waymarked and mostly asphalt cycle tracks.

NATURAL ENVIRONMENT

Physical geography

The Moselle is a left-bank tributary of the Rhine, draining a basin of over 28,000km^2. Its main catchment includes the western side of the Vosges Mountains through tributaries Meurthe, Seille and Saar, and the southern part of the Eifel range through the Sauer and Kyll. In its length of 538km it falls 653m, flows through France for 296km, forms the German–Luxembourg border for 36km, then flows 206km through Germany.

There are three distinct geological parts to the Moselle basin, all shaped by geomorphic events further south approximately 30 million years ago, when the Alps were pushed up by the collision of the African and European tectonic plates. This caused rippling of the landmass to the north, creating successive ridges that form the limestone Jura (northern Switzerland) and Vosges (France). Further north, pre-existing sandstone and slate mountains (Hunsrück) and volcanic remnants (Eifel) were raised further. The Moselle rises high on the western slopes of the Vosges and firstly flows down through the foothills. Secondly, it enters a wide valley between limestone hills filled with tertiary deposits of sand and gravel. Much of this has been extracted for building aggregates, creating a large number of man-made lakes. Finally, when the river reaches the Hunsrück it flows through

The Moselle enters the Rhine at Deutsches Eck in Koblenz (Stage 14)

a deep meandering gorge, caused by the river cutting down through the slate rocks as they were pushed up by the rising Alps.

Wildlife

While a number of small animals (including rabbits, hares, red squirrels, voles, water rats and weasels) may be seen scuttling across the track, and deer glimpsed in forests, this is not a route for observing mammals. However, there is a wide range of interesting birdlife. White swans, geese and many varieties of ducks inhabit the river and its banks. Cruising above, raptors, particularly buzzards and kites, are frequently seen hunting small mammals, with kites diving occasionally into the river to catch fish. Other birds that live by

fishing include cormorants – noticeable when perched on rocks with their wings spread out to dry – and kingfishers. These live in many locations, mostly on backwaters, perching where they can observe the water. Despite their bright blue and orange plumage, they are very difficult to spot. Grey herons, on the other hand, are very visible. Common all along the Moselle, they can be seen standing in shallow water waiting to strike or stalking purposefully along the banks.

PREPARATION

When to go

The route is generally cycleable from mid-April to late October. Indeed, much of the route can be cycled at any time of year, although some of the rougher sections of towpath in Meurthe et Moselle département may be muddy after heavy rain. During July and August (the school holiday season) the popular tourist area through the Moselle gorge between Trier and Cochem (Stages 10–13) can become very busy. However, there is such a wide variety of accommodation available that it is seldom difficult to find somewhere to stay.

How long will it take?

The main route has been broken into 14 stages that average a distance of 36km each, while three variant stages and two one-day excursions visit interesting locations just off the main route. A fit cyclist, cycling an average of 72km per day, should be able to complete the main route in a week. Allowing time for sightseeing, and completing all routes in this guide, cycling the Moselle would make an attractive two-week holiday. There are many places to stay all along the route and it is easy to tailor daily distances to your requirements.

What kind of cycle is suitable?

While most of the route is on asphalt cycle tracks or quiet country roads, there are some stretches of unmade canal towpath with all-weather dirt or gravel surfaces, particularly in Meurthe et Moselle département between Charmes and Méréville (Stage 4, south of Nancy) and between

Pont-à-Mousson and Novéant (Stage 6, north of Nancy). As a result, cycling the route by staying true to the river is not recommended for narrow-tyred racing cycles. There are, however, on-road alternatives for both these stages that can be used to bypass the rougher sections. The most suitable type of cycle is either a touring cycle or a hybrid (a lightweight but strong cross between a touring cycle and a mountain bike, with at least 21 gears). There is no advantage in using a mountain bike. Front suspension is beneficial as it absorbs much of the vibration. Straight handlebars, with bar-ends enabling you to vary your position regularly, are recommended. Make sure your cycle is serviced and lubricated before you start, particularly the brakes, gears and chain.

As important as the cycle is the choice of tyres. Slick road tyres are not suitable and knobbly mountain bike tyres not necessary. What you need is something in-between, with good tread and a slightly wider profile than would be used for everyday cycling. To reduce the chance of punctures choose tyres with puncture-resistant armouring, such as a Kevlar™ band.

GETTING THERE AND BACK

By rail

The start of the route at Col de Bussang (715m) is not directly accessible by train. However, Fellering station (442m) (reached from Mulhouse

Ehrenbreitstein fortress, opposite Koblenz (Stage 14)

by regular local trains, which carry cycles) is only 10km east of the pass, and the ascent is fairly easy. From the west, provided you are happy to double Stage 1, Remiremont station (388m) is 36km away, and the ascent is very gentle. Both of these stations can be reached by connections across the SNCF (French railway) network.

People travelling from the UK can take cycles on Eurostar from London St Pancras (not Ebbsfleet or Ashford) to Paris (Gare du Nord) or Brussels (Midi). Cycles booked in advance travel in dedicated cycle spaces in the baggage compartment of the same train as you. Bookings, which cost £30 for a single journey, can be made through Eurostar baggage (0844 822 5822). Cycles must be checked in at St Pancras Eurostar luggage office (beside the bus drop-off point) at least 40mins before departure. Numbers are limited and if no spaces are available your cycle can be sent as registered baggage (£25). In this case it will travel on the next available train and is guaranteed to arrive within 24hrs. In practice, 80 per cent of the time it will travel on the same train as you. There is no requirement to package or dismantle your cycle. More information may be found at www.eurostar. com.

In Continental Europe, people travelling with cycles face the problem that many of the most convenient long-distance services are operated by high-speed trains that have either limited provision for cycles (French TGV) or no space at all (Thalys service from Paris and Brussels to Köln,

23

and German ICE services). Trains from Paris to Nancy, Strasbourg, Mulhouse, Épinal and Remiremont depart from Gare de l'Est, a short ride from Gare du Nord. Services on this route are operated by TGV or ICE high-speed trains, but there are some trains with reserveable space for cycles. To find out which departures these are, look on the SNCF (French Railways) website (www.voyages-sncf.com). Less complete information is available at www.bikes.sncf.com. Booking for French trains is through the SNCF website or via Rail Europe (www.raileurope.co.uk). From Brussels, conventional EuroCity services with cycle space run three times daily to Mulhouse via Luxembourg and Strasbourg.

Alternative access from the UK is to use Stena Line ferries to reach Hoek van Holland from Harwich or the P&O service to Rotterdam from Hull, then Dutch NS (Dutch Railways) trains to Rotterdam. Here you can connect via Venlo and Dusseldorf with DB (German Railways) services,

with cycle provision, that will take you on to Karlsruhe. From Karlsruhe there are trains to Strasbourg (France) for connections to Mulhouse. On Hoek van Holland ferries, through tickets allow UK travellers leaving from London (or any station in East Anglia) to reach any station in the Netherlands. Booking for German trains can be done at www.bahn.com. Up-to-date information on travelling by train with a bicycle can be found on a website dedicated to worldwide rail travel, 'The man in seat 61', www.seat61.com.

By air

The most convenient airport for the start is Basle–Freiburg–Mulhouse, 6km north-west of Basle, which is served by direct flights from many UK and European airports. Airlines have different requirements regarding how cycles are presented and some, but not all, make a charge – this should be paid when booking, as it is usually greater at the airport. All airlines require tyres

FROM BASLE AIRPORT

From Basle–Freiburg–Mulhouse airport, it is a short (2km) ride to St-Louis-la-Chaussée station, from which local trains run to Mulhouse. Leave the airport terminal building by the exit to France. Follow the service road ahead with car parks L. Pass under a road bridge and turn L at the first roundabout. Continue with car parks L and motorway R and go straight ahead at the next roundabout. Turn R and immediately R again (D12bis), crossing the motorway and entering St-Louis. Follow the road bearing R, pass under a railway bridge and turn immediately L (Rue de la Barrière) to reach the station entrance L.

A novel use of an old bike in Archettes (Stage 2)

to be partially deflated, handlebars turned and pedals removed (loosen pedals beforehand to make them easier to remove at the airport). Most will accept your cycle in a transparent polythene bike-bag, although some insist on the use of a cardboard bike-box. These can be obtained from cycle shops, often for free. You do, however, have the problem of how you get the box to the airport!

By road

The start and finish points at Mulhouse (for Col de Bussang) and Koblenz are sufficiently close to be able to leave a vehicle at one end and return by train with your cycle to collect it after completing the ride. If driving from the UK, the distance from the Channel to Mulhouse is approximately 650km; from the Channel to Koblenz is 500km.

European Bike Express operates a coach service with a dedicated cycle trailer from northern England, picking up en route across England to the Mediterranean, with a drop-off point at Nancy in eastern France. Details and booking are through www.bike-express.co.uk. Trains link Nancy and Strasbourg, with connections on to Mulhouse.

Intermediate access

There are international airports at Metz–Nancy–Lorraine (17km north-east of Pont-à-Mousson; Stage 6), Luxembourg (Stage 9A) and Frankfurt Hahn (which is nowhere near Frankfurt, but is in the Hunsrück Mountains 18km south-east of Enkirch on Stage 12).

Much of the route is closely followed by railway lines. Stations en route are listed in the text and shown on the stage maps.

Onward travel

From Koblenz, DB trains with bicycle accommodation run to stations all over Germany, with international connections available through Frankfurt and Köln. For those traveling to the UK the most direct route would involve using Thalys trains from Köln to Brussels and then Eurostar to London. Unfortunately, as Thalys trains do not carry cycles, this route is not practicable. A better route is to take a train from Koblenz to Trier, then to continue on to Luxembourg and Brussels to connect with Eurostar. Most trains on this route carry cycles.

Alternatively, those bound for the UK can travel via Köln and Venlo (Netherlands) to Rotterdam and Hoek van Holland, from where Stena Line (www.stenaline.co.uk) runs two ferries daily (afternoon and overnight) to Harwich. On overnight sailings, passengers must reserve cabins. From Harwich, trains with cycle provision run to London (Liverpool St) and to Cambridge, where connections to the rest of the UK can be made. In addition, P&O ferries (www.poferries.com) sail every night from Rotterdam (Europoort) to Hull. Reaching the terminal involves travelling by train from Rotterdam station to Maassluis, then crossing the Rhine on the Maassluis–Rozenburg ferry. From the Rozenburg ferry ramp, cyclists can follow LF1 signs through Rozenburg for 2.5km, then turn right

and follow a cycle track on the left of the Europaweg for 9km, which leads to the P&O terminal at berth 5805.

Frequent trains from Koblenz run to Frankfurt International airport (often via a connection at Mainz or Wiesbaden), where there are flights to worldwide destinations. Köln–Bonn airport, which has a wide variety of flights, can also be reached by train from Koblenz.

NAVIGATION

Waymarking

The route described is made up from a number of waymarked cycle routes as well as some unsignposted stretches to link these together. As a result, style and consistency of waymarking varies from country to country and stage to stage. In the introduction to each stage an indication is given of the predominant waymarks followed. The route varies from that waymarked in a few places,

Luxembourg cycle route sign

SUMMARY OF NATIONAL CYCLE ROUTES FOLLOWED	
France	Voie Verte des Hautes Vosges
	Véloroute/Chemin de la Moselle (incomplete)
	Boucles de la Moselle
	Véloroute Charles-le-Téméraire
Luxembourg	Piste cyclable (PC plus number)
Germany	Mosel-Radweg (MR)
	Saar-Radweg
	Rhein-Radweg (RR)

where alternative routes are more suitable than the waymarked route.

In France a number of different routes are followed. Stage 1 from Bussang to Remiremont is excellently waymarked as a voie verte. The route from Golbey, just north of Épinal (Stage 3), all the way to Apach on the Franco–German border (Stage 8) is designated as the Véloroute Charles-le-Téméraire and it is part of a much longer, nationally promoted north–south cycle route across eastern France. As this route is still under development, waymarking is inconsistent and in some parts is

French cycle route signs for (clockwise from top-left): Voie Verte des Hautes Vosges; Véloroute de la Moselle; Chemin de la Moselle; Boucles de la Moselle; Charles-le-Téméraire

German Mosel-Radweg sign

non-existent, although waymarks are more or less continuous north of Metz, where it is also known as the Chemin de la Moselle. The circular route from Nancy to Toul via Neuves-Maisons and back to Nancy via Frouard (see Stages 4, 4A, 5A and 5) is waymarked as *Les Boucles de la Moselle*.

Luxembourg has a network of numbered cycle routes designated as *Piste cyclable* ('PC' plus a number). These are in development, but most sections of the routes described in Stages 8, 9 and 9A are complete and signposted. These follow a mixture of asphalt-surfaced farm lanes, routes following old disused railway lines, dedicated cycle tracks and cycle lanes alongside main roads. Full details of the network, with maps, can be found at www.pch.public.lu.

In Germany, cycle routes along both sides of the Moselle are waymarked as Mosel-Radweg; those along the Saar and Rhine are waymarked as Saar-Radweg and Rhein-Radweg respectively.

Maps

There is no specific series of maps that provides comprehensive coverage of the whole route. For France, sheet 516 of the Michelin map *Alsace, Lorraine* (at a scale of 1:200,000) or sheets 314 and 307 (at a scale of 1:150,000) give an overview of the route across Lorraine without specifically showing cycle routes. As the route is under development, things change frequently and the best way to ascertain the up-to-date position is via the Lorraine tourist office, which publishes a map showing sections open, those under construction and those planned (http://lorraine.voie.verte. free.fr).

For the latter stages between Metz and Koblenz, Esterbauer Bikeline publish a cycling guide (see opposite), which includes strip maps of the route along both sides of the river at 1:75,000. The stretch from Schengen, on the Franco–Luxembourg–German border, to Koblenz, is also covered by a laminated folding strip map of the Mosel-Radweg (sheet 198), published by Publicpress publications (www. publicpress.de). They publish a similar map for the Saar-Radweg (sheet 617). Although these are at 1:50,000, they contain less detail and are less accurate than Bikeline guides.

Various online maps are available to download, at a scale of your choice. Particularly useful is Open Street Map (www.openstreetmap. org), which has a cycle route option showing the route in its entirety, including the planned but not yet constructed stages. This can be a little misleading, as when a track is built it does not always take the exact route originally proposed, and moreover it leaves you to make your own choice of alternative road routes to bypass missing sections.

Guidebooks

Bikeline (www.esterbauer.com) publish a *Radtourenbuch und Karte* (cycle tour guidebook with maps) in both English and German, covering the route from Metz to Koblenz.

Although neither a map nor guidebook, a topographic strip map of the Saar and Mosel from Merzig (Saar) to Koblenz, produced by Rahmelverlag (www.rahmel-verlag. de), gives a good overall impression of the route and makes an attractive souvenir. It is published in a number of languages, including English, and is sold in gift shops along the route.

In the UK, most of these maps and guidebooks are available from leading bookshops including Stanford's, London and The Map Shop, Upton upon Severn. Relevant maps are widely available en route.

ACCOMMODATION

Hotels, inns, guesthouses, and bed & breakfast

For most of the route there is a wide variety of accommodation. The stage descriptions identify places known to have accommodation, but the list is by no means exhaustive. Hotels vary from expensive five-star properties to modest local establishments. Hotels and inns usually offer a full meal service, guesthouses do sometimes. B&Bs, which in Germany can be recognised by a sign *zimmer frei* ('room available'), generally offer only breakfast. Tourist information offices will often telephone for you and make local reservations. After hours, some tourist offices display a sign outside showing local establishments with vacancies. Booking ahead is seldom necessary, except on popular stages in high season, although it is advisable to start looking for accommodation after 1600. Most properties are cycle-friendly and will find a secure overnight place for your pride and joy.

Prices for accommodation in both France and Germany are similar to, or slightly cheaper than, prices in the UK.

Bett+Bike

Bett+Bike (www.bettundbike.de) is a German scheme run by ADFC (German cycling club), which has over 5000 registered establishments providing cycle-friendly accommodation. It includes a wide variety of properties, from major hotels to local B&Bs, listed by state in an annually updated guidebook. Participating establishments display a Bett+Bike sign.

Bett+Bike sign

Youth hostels

There are 13 official youth hostels, many in historic buildings, on or near the route (three French, eight German and two in Luxembourg). These are listed in Appendix E. To use a youth hostel you need to be a member of an association affiliated to Hostelling International. If you are not a member you will be required to join the local association. Rules vary from country to country but generally all hostels accept guests of any age, although visitors over 27 may face a small surcharge (€3 in Germany). Rooms vary from single-sex dormitories to family rooms of two to six beds. Unlike British hostels, most continental European hostels do not have self-catering facilities but do provide good-value hot meals. Hostels can get very busy, particularly during school holidays, and booking is advised through www.hihostels.com.

Camping

If you are prepared to carry camping equipment this may appear the cheapest way of cycling the Moselle. However, good-quality campsites with all facilities are often only a little cheaper than B&Bs or hostels. The stage descriptions identify many official campsites, but the list is by no means exhaustive. Camping may be possible in other locations with the permission of local landowners.

FOOD AND DRINK

Where to eat

There are thousands of places where cyclists can eat and drink, varying from snack bars, hotdog stands and local inns to Michelin-starred restaurants. The locations of many places to eat are identified in the stage descriptions below, but the list is by no means exhaustive. Days and opening times vary. Try to be flexible when planning your day, as a number of inns and small restaurants do not open at lunchtime and may observe one day a week, known in German as *ruhetag*, on which they remain closed. A local inn offering food and drink is typically known as *auberge* in France and *gaststätte* in Germany. A *weinstube* is a winebar, often attached to a vineyard. Some restaurants in big cities and tourist areas may have English-language menus, but these are less common in smaller towns and rural locations.

When to eat

Breakfast in France is usually continental: breads, jam and a hot drink; in Germany it is the same but with the addition of cold meats, cheese and a boiled egg. In Germany lunch was traditionally the main meal of the day, but this is slowly changing, and a large lunch is unlikely to prove suitable if you plan an afternoon in the saddle. The most common lunchtime snacks everywhere are soups or sandwiches. In France *croque monsieur* (toasted ham and cheese sandwich) and *quiche Lorraine* are widely available, while in Germany *wurst mit senf und brot* (sausages with mustard and bread) and *wurst salat* (thin strips of slicing sausage served with *sauerkraut* – pickled cabbage) are popular.

For dinner, a wide variety of cuisine is available. In France cooking is treated almost as a religion, with even the smallest restaurant offering a variety of good-quality dishes cooked on the premises, often using locally sourced ingredients. German cuisine is less varied, but quality is always good and portions are generally large. There are many restaurants offering other options including Italian, Greek, Turkish and Chinese. Much of what is available is pan-European and will be easily recognisable. There are, however, national and regional dishes you may wish to try.

What to eat

In France the route is entirely in Lorraine, which has a typically French cuisine with some Alsatian and

Quiche Lorraine

German influences. This includes the popular Alsatian dish of *choucroute garnie*, a dish of various cuts of pork meat and sausages served with sauerkraut heated in white wine. A typical light meal is *tarte flambée* or *flammekueche*, a thin pizza-style base covered with white cheese, onions and bacon and cooked in a wood oven. The most famous local speciality is quiche Lorraine, an open savoury tart filled with egg, cream and bacon. French *patisseries* (cake shops) offer a mouth-watering selection of cakes and pastries including local specialities like macaroons from Nancy and madeleines. Mirabelles are small golden plums, harvested in August and used to make both fruit tarts and a strong fruit brandy.

Germany is the land of the *schwein* (pig) and pork, gammon, bacon and ham dishes dominate German menus. Traditionally, pork was pot-roasted or grilled rather than fried. There are over 1500 types of German *wurst* (sausage), the most common being *bratwurst* (made from minced pork and served grilled or fried), *wienerwurst* (smoked sausages served boiled, known as frankfurters in English) and *blutwurst* (blood sausage). *Sauerbraten* is marinated roast beef, while *fleischkaese* and *leberkaese* are kinds of meat loaf. *Forelle* (trout) and *lachs* (salmon) are the most popular fish. The most common vegetable accompaniments are sauerkraut and boiled potatoes. *Reibekuchen* are potato pancakes, served with apple

A glass of local Riesling at Piesport (Stage 11)

sauce. *Spargel* (white asparagus) is consumed in huge quantities during *Spargelzeit* (asparagus season), between mid-April and 24 June. Germans tend to eat *kuchen* (cakes) in mid-morning or mid-afternoon and as a result desserts offered with main meals are rather limited, often to just apple strudel or ice cream.

Wine

The Moselle gorge, together with its close neighbours Ruwer and Saar, is one of Germany's major wine-producing regions. The vineyards of the German wine-producing *gebiet* (region) of Mosel (formally known as Mosel-Saar-Ruwer) lie almost as far north as grapes can be persuaded to ripen. Vines, planted on steep, slatey slopes, grow on land unfit for normal agriculture. But despite these conditions they are capable of producing some of Germany's finest white wines. This is made possible by a favourable combination of *terroir* (ground conditions), climate, grape variety and production methods. The vines send roots deep down into the hillside, drawing upon constant supplies of mineral-rich water from far below the surface. South-facing slopes are favoured, where direct sunlight is enhanced by light reflected from the river. Slatey surfaces store the heat of the day, encouraging ripening and deterring early frosts.

The grape most suited to these conditions is the Riesling, which is planted on all the most favourable slopes and produces all the finest wines. At its best, Mosel Riesling can compete with the great wines of the world. Despite having a lower alcohol content, the natural balance between dry slatey acidity and fruitiness gives a flavour that can compete with other fuller-bodied wines. But the price of quality is limited quantity. Riesling is a low-yielding grape compared to Müller-Thurgau, a grape that is equally at home in the conditions but produces a lower-quality wine. Secondary slopes and flat land by the river are mostly planted with this grape. This has had an adverse effect upon worldwide perception of Mosel wine, and German wine in general. Nowhere is this more obvious than in Piesport. Here the great south-facing slope of Goldtröpfchen, which rises behind the village and is planted exclusively with Riesling, produces Piesporter, one of the region's best wines. Opposite, on a flat bend in the river around Michelsberg, there are extensive vineyards of Müller-Thurgau, which produce large quantities of the much cheaper and far inferior Piesporter-Michelsberg. This wine is exported throughout the world and has unfortunately come to be seen by many as 'typical' German white wine.

Historically, most wine production (mainly for German consumption) was dry white wine produced from Riesling and Silvaner grapes. In the 1960s, in order to satisfy a perceived demand for sweeter wines in export markets (particularly the UK

Winningen, home of Germany's oldest wine festival (Stage 14)

and US), considerable acreage of Müller-Thurgau was planted at the expense of Silvaner. However, as the UK wine market developed, tastes became steadily drier and German (usually medium–sweet) wine's share of UK sales has declined significantly. There has been some movement back towards producing drier wines and an alteration to the strict German wine classification rules in 2000 has encouraged this. Nowadays the acreage of Müller-Thurgau declines each year. An older local grape, Elbling, is also grown, although this is mostly used for non-varietal production of *sekt* (sparkling wine).

German wine labels can only show varietals (Riesling for instance) if at least 85 per cent of grapes are from a single variety. If no varietal is shown, the wine is either a blend or even pure Müller-Thurgau. Labels also indicate increasing levels of wine quality, *Tafelwein*, *Landwein*, *Qualitätswein*, and *Prädikatswein* (roughly equivalent to the French designations *Vin de Table*, *Vin de Pays*, *VDQS* and *Appellation Contrôlée*). The best-quality wine (*Prädikatswein*) is further divided into six categories, which tell you little about the characteristics of the wine in the bottle but indicate increasing levels of ripeness of the grapes used. The first three of these (*Kabinett*, *Spätlese* and *Auslese*) can be dry (*trochen*), medium (*halbtrochen*) or sweet (*lieblich*, although this is often not shown on the label) depending upon the production process followed in the winery: basically, a longer fermentation allows more sugar to turn to alcohol, giving a stronger, drier wine, but in practice things are more complicated. The other three descriptions (*Beerenauslese*, *Eiswein* and *Trochenbeerenauslese*) denote sweet dessert wines. Classification changes made in 2000 introduced two categories that are specific to dry wines intended mostly for the export market: 'Classic' is a dry wine made from traditional local grape varieties with an alcohol level of at least 11.5 per cent, and 'Selection', which is another name for a *trochen Auslese*.

Weinorten (wine-producing villages) spread right along the gorge, from the French border to Koblenz, and extend short distances down the Saar and Ruwer valleys. Most villages have a number of vineyard slopes, some on more favourable ground than others, and individual growers have strips of vines in different vineyards. Each grower has their own regime of pruning, weeding and application of pesticides. As a result, when seen from a distance, every vineyard appears as a patchwork of plots. The most renowned 'great first-class vineyards', all on south-facing slopes, tend to be in the middle part of the gorge between Schweich and Zell and include Goldtröpfchen and Domherr in Piesport, Juffer and Sonnenuhr slopes in Brauneberg, Bernkasteler Doctor, Wehlener Sonnenuhr and the Würzgarten, Prälat and Treppchen

Vinothek cooperative wine cellars in St Niklolaus Monastery, Kues (Stage 11)

vineyards between Ürzig and Erden. There is also one in the Saar Valley (Schwarzhofberg) and two in the Ruwer (Karthäuserhofberg and Grünhauser Abtsberg). Other famous vineyards, often with associated local legends include the *Kröver Nacktarsch* (bare bottom), *Zeller Schwarze Katz* (black cat) and *Bullayer Brautrock* (bridal gown). Most *weinorte* have an annual wine festival, the oldest being in Winningen near Koblenz.

Not surprisingly, prices vary from reasonable to very expensive, although you will be surprised at how affordable much of the wine is. Perhaps the best way to sample the various wines is to try a small glass of Kabinett with a lunchtime snack and a Spätlese or Auslese with your evening meal (ask for trochen if you want dry!). To go the whole hog, you could finish with an after dinner glass of sweet dessert wine – ask for Trochenbeerenauslese. One way to compare a wide variety of wines at one time is to buy a €15 sampling ticket at the Vinothek, a co-operative wine merchant in the cellars of the Cusanus St Nikolaus monastery in Kues (Stage 11), where you can taste over 100 wines.

Other parts of the Moselle valley also produce wine. Lorraine was once a major wine-producing region, but after the industry was wiped out by the 19th-century phylloxera epidemic, little replanting was carried out. Nowadays production is limited to a small area around Metz and a larger area around Toul (Côtes de Toul) that is best known for Vin Gris, a rosé wine made from a blend of Gamay, Pinot Noir and local white grape varieties. In Luxembourg wine is produced all along the Moselle, with Rivaner (a local name for Müller-Thurgau) being the dominant, although declining, grape. The best-known wine is Crémant de Luxembourg, a champagne-style sparkling wine.

Beer and other beverages

Although the part of the country through which the Moselle flows is a wine-producing and -consuming region, Germany is predominantly a beer-drinking nation. France, by contrast, is a wine-drinking nation where consumption of beer is higher in northern and eastern regions, including Lorraine. In Germany, purity laws controlling the production and content of beer have limited the mass consolidation of brewing compared to other European countries, beer still being brewed in a large number of local breweries. Lager and pilsner are the most widely drunk forms, although *weizenbier* (wheat beer), found in both *helles* (pale) and *dunkles* (dark) varieties, is growing in popularity. Very refreshing and slightly sweet tasting, wheat beer is unfiltered and thus naturally cloudy. Glass sizes vary, but common sizes are *kleines* (small, 300ml) and *grosses* (large, half-litre). Weizenbier is traditionally served in half-litre vase-shaped glasses. *Radler* in Germany is shandy, a 50/50 mix of beer and carbonated lemonade. With a long history of German influence, Alsace and Lorraine are the main beer-producing regions of France, and a wide variety of beers are available. *Blanche* is wheat beer similar to German weizenbier, while *blonde* is a pale-coloured lager.

All the usual soft drinks (including colas, lemonade, fruit juices and mineral waters) are widely available. Apple juice mixed 50/50 with carbonated water, known as *apfelschorle*, is widely consumed in Germany. *Cidre* (France), *apfelwein* and viez (Germany) are cider-like alcoholic drinks produced from apples. Tap water is safe to drink everywhere.

AMENITIES AND SERVICES

Grocery shops

All cities, towns and larger villages passed through have grocery shops, many have supermarkets and most have pharmacies. Opening hours vary, but grocers in Germany close at 1300 on Saturdays and stay closed all day Sunday. In France they may be closed from 1300 to 1600 daily.

Cycle shops

The route is well-provided with cycle shops, most of which offer repair facilities. Locations are identified in the stage descriptions, although the list is not exhaustive. Many cycle shops will adjust brakes and gears, or lubricate your chain, while you wait, often not seeking reimbursement for minor repairs. Touring cyclists should not abuse this generosity and always offer to pay, even if payment is refused.

Currency and banks

France, Germany and Luxembourg switched from national currencies to the Euro (€) in 2002. Almost every town has a bank and most have ATM machines that enable you to make transactions in English. Travellers from the UK should contact their banks to confirm activation of bank cards for use in continental Europe.

Telephone and internet

The whole route has mobile phone (*handy*, in German) coverage. Contact your network provider to ensure your phone is enabled for foreign use with the optimum price package. To make an international call dial the international access code of the country you are in (00 or + in the UK), followed by the dialling code for the country you wish to reach:

- **+33** France
- **+352** Luxembourg
- **+49** Germany
- **+44** UK

Most hotels, guesthouses and hostels make internet access available to guests, often free but sometimes for a small fee.

Electricity

Voltage is 220v, 50Hz AC. Plugs are standard European two-pin round.

WHAT TO TAKE

Clothing and personal items
Although the route is predominantly downhill, weight should be kept to a minimum. You will need clothes for cycling (shoes, socks, shorts or trousers, shirt, fleece and waterproofs) and clothes for evenings and days off. The best maxim is two of each: 'one to wear, one to wash'. The time of year makes a difference, as you'll need more and warmer clothing in April–May and in September–October. All clothing should be able to be washed en route, and a small tube or bottle of travel wash is useful. A sunhat and sunglasses are essential, while gloves and a woolly hat are advisable, except in high summer.

In addition to your usual toiletries you will need sun cream and lip salve. You should take a simple first-aid kit. If staying in hostels you will need a towel and a torch (your cycle light should suffice).

Cycle equipment
Everything you take needs to be carried on your cycle. If overnighting in accommodation, a pair of rear panniers should be sufficient to carry all your clothing and equipment; if camping you may also need front panniers. Panniers should be completely watertight. If in doubt, pack everything inside a strong polythene lining bag. Rubble bags, obtainable from builders' merchants, are ideal for this purpose. A bar-bag is a useful way

Fully loaded cycle at the Moselle's source (Stage 1)

of carrying items you need to access quickly such as maps, sunglasses, camera, spare tubes, puncture repair kit and tools. A transparent map case attached to the top of your bar-bag is an ideal way of displaying a map and guidebook.

Your cycle should be fitted with mudguards and a bell, and be capable of carrying water bottles, a pump and lights. Many cyclists fit an odometer to measure distances. A basic toolkit should consist of puncture repair kit, spanners, Allen keys, adjustable spanner, screwdriver, spoke key and chain repair tool. The only spares worth carrying are two spare tubes (which are essential) and spare spokes. On a long cycle ride, sometimes on dusty tracks, your chain will need regular lubrication and you should either carry a can of spray-lube or make regular visits to cycle shops. A good strong lock is advisable.

Weather

The route of the Moselle runs along the boundary between the continental climate zone, typified by warm dry summers interspersed with short periods of heavy rain and cold winters, and the Atlantic coastal weather zone, with cooler summers, milder winters and more frequent but lighter periods of precipitation carried by a prevailing westerly wind. The beginning of Stage 1 is exposed to mountain weather with heavy winter snowfall, but this melts in most years by mid-April.

Road safety

Throughout the route, cycling is on the right side of the road. If you have never cycled on the right before you will adapt quickly, but roundabouts may prove challenging. You are most prone to mistakes when setting off in

AVERAGE TEMPERATURES (MAX/MIN DEGREES C)						
	Apr	May	Jun	Jul	Aug	Sep	Oct
Bussang	14/2	18/6	20/9	22/11	21/11	19/7	14/4
Metz	15/5	20/9	23/12	25/14	25/14	20/10	15/7
Koblenz	15/4	20/8	22/11	25/13	25/13	20/10	15/6

AVERAGE RAINFALL (MM/RAINY DAYS)						
	Apr	May	Jun	Jul	Aug	Sep	Oct
Bussang	43/NA	56/NA	71/NA	66/NA	71/NA	61/NA	46/NA
Metz	51/9	59/10	62/10	64/9	61/9	64/9	72/11
Koblenz	47/10	66/10	74/11	75/10	59/9	60/10	59/10

NA: *information not available*

the morning. In France the general rule is to allow priority to traffic coming from the right, unless otherwise indicated. One-way streets often have signs permitting contra-flow cycling.

Much of the route is on dedicated cycle tracks, although care is necessary as these are sometimes shared with pedestrians. Use your bell, politely, when approaching pedestrians from behind. Where you are required to cycle on the road, there is usually a dedicated cycle lane.

Many city and town centres have pedestrian-only zones. These restrictions are often only loosely enforced and you may find locals cycling within them – indeed, many zones have signs showing cycling is allowed.

None of the countries passed through require the compulsory wearing of cycle helmets, although their use is recommended. Modern lightweight helmets with improved ventilation have made wearing them more comfortable.

Emergencies

In the unlikely event of an accident the standardised EU emergency phone number is 112. The entire route has mobile phone coverage. Provided you have a European Health Insurance Card (EHIC) issued by your home country (for the UK, search 'EHIC' at www.nhs.uk), medical costs for EU citizens are covered under reciprocal health insurance agreements, although you may have to pay for an ambulance and claim the cost back later through insurance.

Insurance

Travel insurance policies usually cover you when cycle touring but they do not normally cover damage to, or theft of, your bicycle. If you have a household contents policy, it may cover cycle theft, but limits may be less than the real cost of your cycle. The Cycle Touring Club (CTC; www.ctc.org.uk) offers a policy tailored for your needs when cycle touring.

ABOUT THIS GUIDE

Text and maps

There are 19 route descriptions, each covered by separate maps drawn to a scale of 1:150,000. At this scale it is not practical to cycle the route using only these maps, and more detailed local maps are advised. However, apart from stages in Meurthe et Moselle département, signposting and waymarking is generally good and, using these combined with the stage descriptions, it should be possible to cycle much of the route without the expense or weight of a large number of other maps. Beware, however, as the route described here does not always follow the waymarked route.

Place names on the maps that are significant for route navigation are shown in **bold** in the text. Distances shown are cumulative within each stage. Altitudes are approximate as,

The River Leuk's pretty waterfall in the middle of Saarburg (Excursion 1)

following the river, the route often passes slightly below the point in each town where official altitude is calculated and an estimate has been made of altitude reached. For each city, town and village passed an indication is given of facilities available (accommodation, refreshments, YH, camping, tourist office, cycle shop, station) when the guide was written. These lists are neither exhaustive nor do they guarantee that establishments are still in business. No attempt has been made to list all such facilities, as this would require another book the same size as this one. For a full listing of accommodation, contact local tourist offices and/or search online. Tourist offices in principle cities and towns along the route are listed in Appendix D.

Below Neuves-Maisons (Stage 4A), large black-on-white number boards show kilometre distance along the navigable course above Deutsches Eck (Koblenz), where the Moselle joins the Rhine. Where these are shown in the text, they appear in bold as **Mkm** (**Skm** on the Saar, **Rkm** on the Rhine).

While the route descriptions are accurate at the time of writing, things do change. Between Épinal (Stage 2) and Thionville (Stage 7), construction work is ongoing to create a continuous cycle route. While this is generally complete in Vosges and Moselle départements, much work remains to be done in the département of Meurthe et Moselle. This may lead to temporary diversions of the route, or, as new stretches of cycle track are completed, permanent re-routing. Watch out for signs (often only in local languages) showing such alterations.

Some alternative routes exist and where these offer a reasonable variant, usually because of a better surface, they are described in the text and shown on the maps.

Language

The French spelling of Moselle (which is the same as the English spelling) is used throughout the introduction and for Stages 1–9, which run through France. For Stages 10–14 the German spelling Mosel is used. Place names, street names and points of interest are given in appropriate local languages. In German ß (known as an *eszett*) is expressed as double 'ss'. Nouns and their descriptive adjectives are often run together to form longer words. Where this occurs, it is reflected in the text.

STAGE 1

Col de Bussang to Remiremont

Start	Col de Bussang, Moselle source (715m)
Finish	Remiremont, Rue des 5ème et 15ème BCP (388m)
Distance	36km
Waymarking	Voie Verte des Hautes Vosges (Bussang to Remiremont)

The first stage of the route is a steady descent, mostly on an asphalt cycle track. It runs along the route of a disused railway, and passes a series of small communities that have a history of silver and copper mining. The Moselle grows from a tiny stream to a fast-flowing river, as it leads through a picturesque valley with the thickly wooded foothills of the Vosges Mountains on both sides.

The Moselle cycle route begins at the river's source, so those who start from Fellering station first need to complete 10km of fairly easy ascent to the Col de Bussang.

From Fellering to the source

From **Fellering** station (442m), go straight ahead along the station approach road SW away from the railway. Pass a church L and turn R on the main road (D13b). Turn first L (Rue des Écoles) and after 200m bear L to cross a river. Turn R (Rue des Saules) and, at the end, turn L at a T-junction. After 50m, bear R on Chemin du See and follow this WSW, bearing R out of Fellering and passing a seasonal lake below L to reach **Urbès** (3km, 450m). At the beginning of the village, keep L (do not follow signs uphill R) then bear L at a road junction (following Rue du Brisgau) and turn R (easily missed) after 100m (Rue Gassel). Follow the road as it bears L to reach the N66 road at a T-junction. ▶

The N66 is a main road without cycle lanes and, although it is not very busy, care is needed.

Turn R and follow the N66, climbing up into the Vosges through forest, gaining height by a series of seven hairpins, to reach a moto-hotel at the **Col de Bussang** (731m) (accommodation, refreshments). This was the

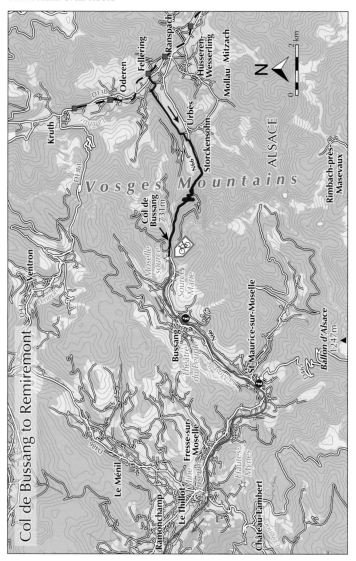

border crossing point between Germany and France from 1871 to 1919. Continue over the col for 300m. Fork R onto the D89 to reach, after 200m, the **Moselle source** L (10km, 715m).

The source of the Moselle, near Col de Bussang

> The official **source of the Moselle** is a spring just below Col de Bussang. This, however, is fed by several streams rising above the 1000m contour, on the slopes of Grand Drumont, which disappear below ground and re-emerge at the source.
>
> A sign proclaims that it is 550km from here by river to Koblenz. The actual length is variously quoted between 534km and 550km, depending upon the measurement of meanders cut-off by the process of canalisation. The most accurate measure seems to be 538km. A relief in the stonework surrounding the spring graphically shows the route you are to follow. A plaque displays a line from the poem *Mosella*, dedicated to the river by the fourth-century Roman poet Ausonius: *O Moselle salut!*

Mère illustre en produit en jeunesse guerrière et en hommes instruits ('a toast to the Moselle, renowned mother of bellicose youth and knowledgeable men').

The main route begins by following the D89 downhill from the **source**, with the Moselle appearing as a tiny stream on the R. Cross the stream by a bridge and continue gently downhill past a number of farms and scattered houses, with the infant Moselle feeding a series of small lakes and ponds L. Continue through the hamlet of Les Sources, passing **la source Marie** L, a hexagonal building containing a natural mineral water spring said to be good for health. Pass a turning R leading to Bussang ski resort (visible on the hillside R) and continue ahead to reach **Bussang** (3km, 598m) (accommodation, refreshments, camping, tourist office).

Bussang (pop. 1800) nestles beneath the Vosges Mountains in the upper Moselle valley on the route of a Roman road from Basle to Metz. The village developed around modest silver mines. Mineral water springs with a high iron content were discovered and led to it becoming a spa resort for the treatment of anaemia and the production of bottled mineral water. Bacteriological contamination led to three of the four springs closing and production of mineral water ceased in 1971. Ongoing attempts have been made to drill a new uncontaminated source but this has been bogged down by political arguments.

However, Bussang remains a year-round resort with winter sports, summer walking and a small casino. The Théâtre du Peuple, which opened in 1895, is constructed entirely of wood and is unusual for the fact that its backdrop can be completely opened in order to provide performances with a natural upstage scene of woods and mountains.

Pass a hospital R and dogleg R then L across the N66 into a small road. Bear R through the casino car park L

and continue between another car park R and the reno-
vated Bussang station L, which now houses the tourist
office. Turn L at a T-junction and, after 50m, R onto the
Voie Verte des Hautes Vosges cycle track along the course
of a disused railway line. ▶ Initially heading SW, the
track skirts **St Maurice-sur-Moselle** (7km, 554m) (accommodation, refreshments, camping, tourist office).

The start of the Voie Verte des Hautes Vosges at Bussang

This runs for 33km all the way to Remiremont.

> **St Maurice-sur-Moselle** (pop. 1450) is overlooked
> by one of the highest points in the Vosges range,
> Ballon d'Alsace (1247m), which has an equestrian
> statue of Joan of Arc on its summit. The road over
> the mountain was the scene of the first ever moun-
> tain climb in the Tour de France cycle race (1905),
> and its last use as part of the race was in 2005,
> to celebrate the climb's centenary. A rail tunnel
> beneath the Vosges to Urbès was never completed.

The Voie Verte then turns NW, keeping to the L of
the river, and passes **Fresse-sur-Moselle** (11km, 511m)
(accommodation, refreshments, camping) and **Le Thillot**
(13km, 495m) (accommodation, refreshments, camping),
both on the opposite side of the river.

LE THILLOT

Le Thillot (pop. 4000) was an important mining town founded in the 16th century when the Duke of Lorraine encouraged development of copper mining in the upper Moselle valley. To process the ore, a smelter was built in St Maurice. However, problems arose with the provision of food and merchandise for the mine and smelter employees, in what was a very remote location.

In 1560, the Duke licensed a weekly market in Le Thillot, setting in train a process by which the town became the principal commercial community in the valley. In common with other markets in mining districts of Lorraine, market rules were specifically written to accommodate the needs of the mining community. The market operated on Saturdays only, opening at 1000 to give miners time to reach it after coming off an eight-hour night shift. Moreover, the first hour's trading was reserved for miners, smelters and other workers associated with the mining industry. Traders were not allowed to make transactions on the way to market and were required to ensure that the best and freshest produce, particularly meat, was available for miners. A sign was displayed to indicate when this rule was in force. As the miners were mostly illiterate, this was a reproduction of the ducal arms mounted on the end of a spear. Heavy fines were applied to traders and non-miners caught flouting the regulations.

Copper mining peaked in the 17th century and production continued in Le Thillot until 1761. The mines were the first in Europe to use gunpowder, which before then had only been used for military purposes, to blast rocks. The Hautes-Mynes have reopened as a tourist attraction, where it is possible to visit some of the shafts and galleries. Tickets are available from the mine museum in the old station, but the mines are a steep 3km away in nearby hills.

The track continues to **Ramonchamp** (16km, 472m) (accommodation, refreshments, camping).

The site of a Roman camp – its name is derived from *Romanici Campus* – **Ramonchamp** (pop. 2000) was the principal town of the valley prior to the 16th-century development of Le Thillot. When Prussians annexed Alsace and part of Lorraine at the end of the Franco–Prussian war (1871), French textile manufacturers relocated as refugees to the

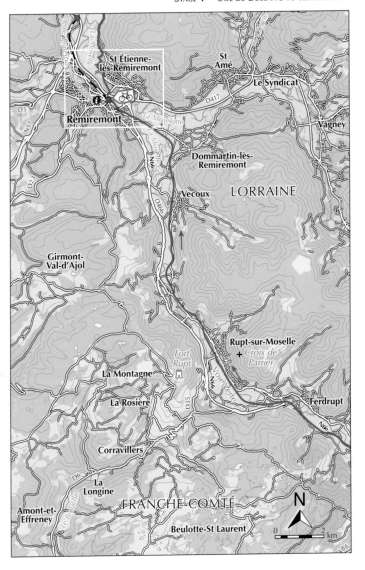

parts of Lorraine that were remaining under French control, including Ramonchamp, which became a flourishing textile-producing town until the decline of the textile industry in the latter half of the 20th century. The town was severely damaged during heavy fighting between retreating German and advancing American forces in late 1944, and was subsequently rebuilt.

After 5km the track crosses the river and continues NW through **Rupt-sur-Moselle** (23.5km, 424m) (accommodation, refreshments, tourist office, cycle shop).

Another small industrial town once home to a flourishing textile industry, **Rupt-sur-Moselle** (pop. 3650) is positioned in a narrow part of the valley, and the hills on either side pay testimony to the frequent conflicts between France and Germany that have swept this region. On the hillside south

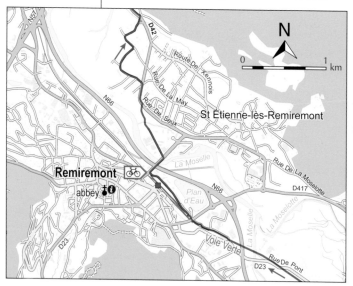

The Abbess's residence in Remiremont

of the town is Fort Rupt, one of a chain of forts constructed to deter further German advances after French defeat in the Franco–Prussian war, while on a hillside north of town is le Croix de Parrier, a 10m-high white concrete cross that is lit at night. This was erected in 1939 as a peace memorial dedicated to those involved in the First World War. Originally due to be inaugurated in the summer of 1939, problems with the lighting delayed consecration until October, by which time the Second World War had begun.

Continue N on the Voie Verte past Maxonchamp (camping) and **Vecoux** (30.5km, 403m). The track skirts **Dommartin-lès-Remiremont** – where it is joined at a roundabout (33km) by another cycle track that has followed a disused railway line down the Moselotte valley – then turns NW, recrossing the river and passing under a motorway to reach the outskirts of Remiremont.

Continue on a cycle track, parallel to Rue du Lit d'Eau on the R, pass under a road bridge and reach a

51

roundabout. Continue ahead on a cycle track between Rue du Lit d'Eau L and a car park, parallel to a railway line with the station L, to reach the end of the stage at Rue des 5ème et 15ème BCP. Turn R to continue onto Stage 2, or L to reach the historic centre of **Remiremont** (36km, 388m) (accommodation, refreshments, tourist office, cycle shop, station).

REMIREMONT

Remiremont (pop. 8000) straddles the Moselle below the confluence of the Moselotte and is surrounded by forest-clad hills. From 910, Remiremont Abbey (originally founded by Benedictines in 620) housed a chapter of noble-born 'canonesses' (nuns) and was the most renowned nunnery in Europe for its wealth and recruitment of canonesses, who had to show 200 years of royal or noble lineage (mostly, presumably, unmarriageable daughters). Enriched by the Dukes of Lorraine, Kings of France and Holy Roman Emperors, the abbey wielded great power and influence, with the abbess, who was consecrated personally by the Pope, holding title as a princess of the Holy Roman Empire. This power was demonstrated by a requirement that the Duke of Lorraine had to swear an oath to protect the independence of the abbey, rather than the canonesses having to swear allegiance to the Duke. To show off this independence the abbey displayed escutcheons (shields) showing the imperial eagle and not the badge of Lorraine.

During the War of Escutcheons (1566), the Duke of Lorraine removed these shields by force and established supremacy over the abbey. By the 17th century, power had fallen away so much that canonesses were allowed to renounce their vows and marry while remaining titular members of the order. The abbey was finally suppressed during the French Revolution. The 13th-century abbey church (with 11th-century crypt) still stands, together with some canonesses' houses, where nuns lived within the abbey close, in their own properties and with a retinue of servants.

The abbess's residence, rebuilt first in 1750 and again, to its original design, after a fire in 1871, now houses the town hall, court house and library. In recent years Remiremont has become known for its range of street fountains, which are mostly of large and complex designs. Local fare includes trout pâté, trout fillets marinated in white wine – eaten hot – goose, gingerbread cupcakes and *lorikeet* (star-shaped marzipan) cakes.

STAGE 2
Remiremont to Épinal

Start	Remiremont, Rue des 5ème et 15ème BCP (388m)
Finish	Épinal, pedestrian bridge (326m)
Distance	28.5km
Waymarking	None (follow the D42)

This stage follows a gently undulating country road through a number of small agricultural villages, never far from the widely meandering Moselle. The gradually widening valley is lined by rolling wooded hillsides. No cycle lane is needed, as the road is very quiet.

Leave **Remiremont** on Rue des 5ème et 15ème BCP. Cross the motorway and the Moselle and turn immediately L (Rue des Poncées). At the end of the road continue ahead on a cycle track past fields (Chemin des Barranges). Bear

Remiremont has a number of arcaded streets

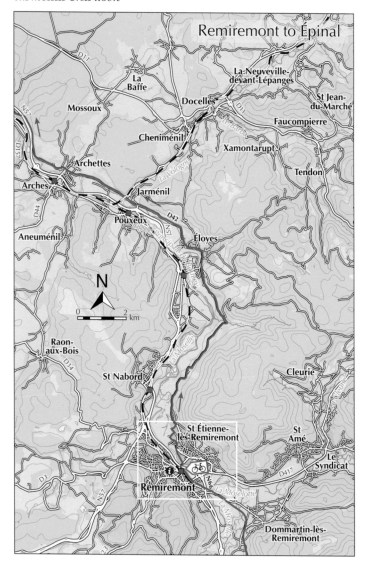

Remiremont to Épinal

L into Rue de Seux and after 200m fork L (Chemin de Pétinchamp). Follow this as it bears R and at a T-junction turn L into Chemin du Chazal. Follow this, bearing R, to reach a crossroads with the main road (D42) in Seux (2km, 387m) (refreshments). Turn L and follow the main road (no cycle lane) as it winds and undulates for 8km between wooded hills R and water meadows L, to reach **Éloyes** (10km, 384m) (accommodation, refreshments, station).

Cliffs overhang the D42 near Archettes

Follow the D42 (Rue des Donjons) straight ahead through the village and bear L into Rue de Jarménil (still the D42). Continue, with the river now nearer L, to reach a roundabout just after entering **Jarménil** (14km, 366m) (station). Take the second exit, continuing on the main road as it bypasses the village. Cross a bridge over La Vologne river and follow the D42, bearing L under a railway bridge, continuing to **Archettes** (17.5km, 351m) (station).

Stone statue near Éloyes

Stay on the D42 (Route d'Épinal) through the village and continue, with the river L and wooded hillsides with strangely gnarled cliff faces overhanging the road R. Pass under a motorway and follow the Moselle around a bend

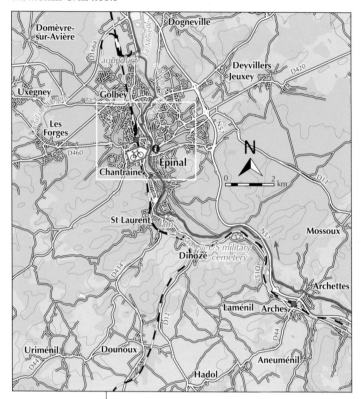

to the L, with a brief glimpse of the US flag flying over the **Dinoze** US military cemetery on a bluff above the river R (22km).

Situated near Dinoze on the opposite bank, on a bluff 30m above the river, is a **US military cemetery**, holding 5255 graves and a memorial to a further 424 combatants missing in action. They were mostly members of the US 7th Army, which landed in southern France on 15 August 1944 and moved north to reach and liberate Épinal in September, before crossing the Rhine near Worms in March 1945 and advancing through southern Germany. Many of the dead were killed during heavy fighting in the Heasbourg gap during the winter of 1944–1945.

In May 1958, 13 caskets, containing the remains of an unidentified combatant from each US military cemetery in Europe, were brought to Dinoze. One was selected randomly and sent to a further selection ceremony held on a destroyer in the mid-Atlantic. Here, one casket was chosen from all the theatres of war to be reinterred at Arlington National Cemetery in Washington DC, as the tomb of the Unknown Soldier.

Continue on the D42 (Route d'Archettes) to reach the outskirts of Épinal. Fork L at a roundabout, following the river past a **dam** and a large disused mill complex on the opposite bank, L. Continue around a long sweeping river bend, past a car components factory R to reach a road junction. Turn L onto a cycle track running between the road and river, and continue past a bridge over the Moselle L.

The US military cemetery at Dinoze

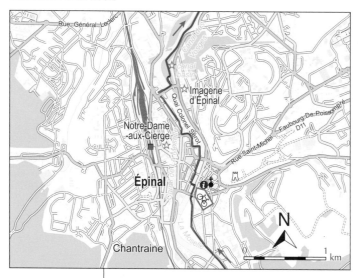

The ruins of Épinal castle

Pass a series of car parks and the Parc du Cours L. Pass around another car park to reach a crossroads with Pont Sadi Carnot bridge L and the modern Prefecture des Vosges local government building R. Continue ahead to reach the next bridge – a modern combined pedestrian and cycle bridge with a plexiglas canopy that marks the end of the stage. Turn L over the Moselle to continue onto Stage 3 or turn R to reach the old centre of **Épinal** (28.5km, 326m) (accommodation, refreshments, camping, tourist office, cycle shop, station).

ÉPINAL

Épinal (pop. 35,400) is an ancient town that developed around a castle built on a rocky spur overlooking the Moselle, and is now *prefecture* (county town) of Vosges département. The old town contains the Place des Vosges, Chapitre district, St Maurice Basilica and the remains of the medieval castle. On 9 September 1811 Napoleon addressed his troops in Épinal prior to departure for their ill-fated attack on Russia. Local legend has it that his ghost walks the ramparts at 0500 every year on that day.

The Franco–Prussian war had two major effects upon the town. Firstly, between 1871 and 1914 it was heavily fortified as one of four strongholds of the Séré de Rivières defence line (with Toul, Belfort and Verdun), which was aimed at protecting France from further German advances, and by 1913 there were 30,000 troops stationed in the town. Secondly, when Germany occupied Alsace in 1870, many industrialists from Mulhouse relocated their businesses to Épinal, boosting the textile industry.

The town's most famous products are *Imagerie d'Épinal* (Épinal Prints); these were first produced by Jean-Charles Pellerin in 1796 and they became very popular collectors' items in 19th-century France. The company is still operating today, using traditional printing methods to produce stencilled woodblock prints depicting historical or religious subjects, storybook characters, Napoleonic history, military subjects and other folk themes in bright colours. Near the station, the outwardly nondescript concrete church of Notre-Dame-aux-Cierge has a rear wall constructed entirely of stained glass, which bathes the interior in blue and red light.

STAGE 3
Épinal to Charmes

Start	Épinal, pedestrian bridge (326m)
Finish	Charmes, Place Henri Breton (284m)
Distance	28km
Waymarking	None, but the route follows the Canal des Vosges throughout

This stage follows a steadily widening valley, with wooded hills now set further back from the river. A lot of land near the Moselle has been used for aggregate extraction; this has left several areas of water, many of which are now used for recreational purposes. With a few short gravel sections, a nearly continuous asphalt cycle path follows the Canal des Vosges all the way from Épinal to Charmes. This canal allows small boats to reach Épinal, the head of navigation.

The Épinal branch of the Canal des Vosges, where the cycle route follows the towpath

Cross the plexiglas-roofed combined pedestrian and cycle bridge over the Moselle in the middle of **Épinal**. Immediately after crossing the bridge turn R on a cycle track between Quai Louis Lapicque and the river.

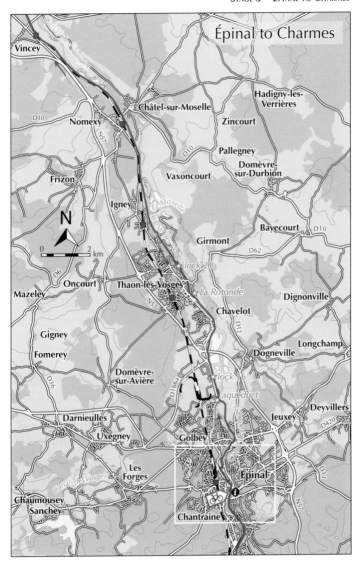

Continue ahead alongside Quai Maréchal de Contades and follow this, bearing L away from the river (Rue de Verdun). Turn R at a crossroads (Rue de la Chipotte) and follow this, bearing L, with a monument to the French resistance movement R. Cross an old canal, now used for white-water canoeing, and turn sharply R beside a red British telephone box on a cycle track that winds through gardens with a car park L. Continue through a gap in a wall into a small rose garden in front of a building known as the Roman house. At the end of the rose garden continue ahead through a gateway into a narrow road between high walls (Impasse des Blanchisseuses) and drop down L to join a gravel cycle track. Just before the end of the track, fork L to pass under a road bridge and bear R to reach Ave de la Republique. Continue ahead across the Moselle on a cycle track L of the road.

Turn L after the bridge onto a road into a car park. ◄ At the end turn R then bear L on a cycle track through an open grassy area between the Moselle L and the **canal basin** R. This was previously the commercial quay of Épinal and it marks the limit of navigation for the Moselle. Continue on a gravel track between the Canal des Vosges R and the river L, pass under a road bridge and continue ahead along the towpath. Cross the river on an **aqueduct** and turn immediately L, dropping down to join an asphalt path beside the river. Turn sharply L

To visit Imagerie d'Épinal, continue ahead after crossing the bridge and turn R at the roundabout.

The canal aqueduct over the Moselle near Épinal

under the aqueduct and continue for 250m to reach a road. Cross this road and turn R on the towpath, passing a sewage works and aggregates plant (both R), to reach **lock 16**. Continue beside the canal on the towpath, passing a lagoon R, and reach lock 17. Pass an aggregates quay L and follow the towpath under a motorway bridge. Continue ahead on a track between a lagoon R and the canal L to reach lock 18 at **Chavelot** (8km, 307m) (accommodation, refreshments), with the Moselle R.

The route continues on the canal towpath, passing **La Rotonde** sports and community centre beside lock 19. Immediately after the lock, climb up to the road, and turn L then L again to drop down on the opposite canal bank. Turn L under a bridge to continue on the towpath on the other side of the canal, passing **Thaon-les-Vosges** L (10km, 303m) (accommodation, refreshments, station).

> **Thaon-les-Vosges** (pop. 8250) is an industrial town that developed after the relocation of the textile industry from Alsace in 1871. The major employer was La Blanchisserie et Teinturerie de Thaon (BTT), which ran a huge bleaching and dyeing factory that employed over 3000 at its peak. Decline of the textile industry in the latter part of the 20th century led to closure in 2003. The company has left a legacy for the town in the form of the impressive Rotonde, a social centre developed by BTT for its employees and now used as a local community centre. The factory site is being redeveloped into smaller industrial units.

Pass under a road bridge, then at **lock 20** recross the canal and turn L along the towpath; follow this for 16km towards Charmes. Soon after lock 21 the path doglegs around an aggregates quay and then returns to the canal bank to pass a series of locks including **Igney** (lock 22) (14km, 294m) (station) and **Nomexy** (lock 25) (18km, 285m) (station), both on the other side of the canal. At **Vincey** (lock 28) (23km, 277m) (accommodation, refreshments, station), the towpath follows the canal under a

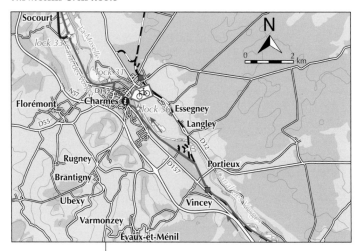

To bypass Charmes, stay on the E side of the canal at lock 30 and continue along the towpath to join Stage 4 at lock 31 (see p66).

railway bridge, and then passes a large disused factory L. Another disused factory is passed, this time R, by lock 29. ◄ To visit Charmes, cross the canal at **lock 30** (Pont le Courtrey), cross the millstream and turn R uphill (Bd Nestor Eury), then turn R again (D157, Rue Maurice Barres) to reach the end of the stage at Place Henri Breton in **Charmes** (28km, 284m) (accommodation, refreshments, camping, tourist office, station).

La Rotonde community centre in Thaon-les-Vosges

Charmes town hall

CHARMES

Charmes (pop. 4500) has been a frequent casualty of centuries-long struggles, firstly between Lorraine and France, and latterly between France and Prussia then France and Germany. The town has been captured and destroyed by invading forces four times in 500 years, first by Burgundians (1475), then by the French during the Thirty Years' War (1635).

Charmes, along with the rest of Lorraine, became French in 1766. There followed a century of prosperity, with Charmes developing into a small industrial town with its principal industries of tanning and brewing being driven by ample supplies of water from the Vosges. Destroyed again by the Prussians during the Franco–Prussian war, and then rebuilt, the town was the site of a key battle at the beginning of the First World War (1914). The German army tried to break through French defensive lines between the fortified towns of Épinal and Toul – the so-called 'Gap of Charmes'. Three days of heavy fighting resulted in a French victory, after which the Lorraine front became stalemated for the rest of the war. This battle is commemorated by the 13m-high Lorraine monument, which stands on a hillside above the town. Towards the end of the Second World War, the retreating German army completely destroyed the town for the fourth time in its history on 5 September 1944. Rebuilding took five years, from 1947 to 1952.

STAGE 4
Charmes to Nancy

Start	Charmes, Place Henri Breton (284m)
Finish	Nancy, Rue Molitor (196m)
Distance	47.5km
Waymarking	None to Méréville, then Boucles de la Moselle to Nancy

A wide agricultural valley, with many man-made lakes and lagoons continues as far as Méréville, beyond which a low ridge blocks the valley and forces the Moselle to flow west through a wooded gorge (the variant Stage 4A follows the Moselle from Méréville, bypassing Nancy). South of Méréville, very little development has been made in terms of providing asphalt cycle tracks and where the canal towpath is useable it is mostly gravel, rough stone or bare earth, but a road that parallels the main route provides a suitable alternative. Beyond Méréville the main route climbs gently over the ridge, following the well-signposted and -surfaced Boucles de la Moselle cycle route; it leads along towpaths beside the Canal de Jonction and Canal de la Marne au Rhin to run into the centre of Nancy.

Those on Stage 3 who choose to bypass Charmes join Stage 4 here.

To rejoin the canal, leave Place Henri Breton in **Charmes** on rue des Capucins (continuation through town of Rue Maurice Barres) and turn third R (Rue de l'Écluse). Follow this over a canal bridge by **lock 31** and turn L on a track parallel with the towpath, passing a shooting club R. ◄ Beyond lock 32, this track joins the towpath as far as **lock 33**.

Alternative route for touring cycles
Beyond lock 33, where the route enters Meurthe et Moselle département, the track becomes inconsistent and parts may not be suitable for touring cycles. For an alternative route, cross the canal at lock 33 and turn R along the D570 for the next 26km, initially passing **Socourt** and **Gripport**. Continue through **Bainville-aux-Miroirs**,

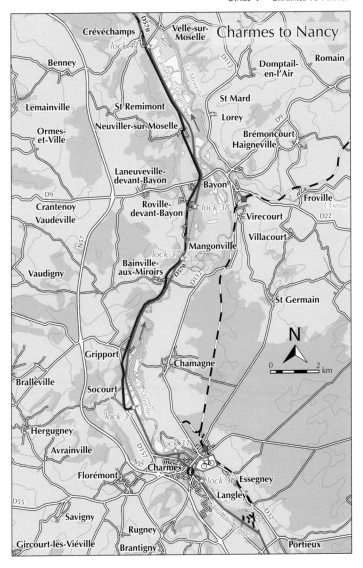

Mangonville (where the alternative and main route rejoin as one for a short section), **Roville-devant-Bayon** and **Neuviller-sur-Moselle** and pass **Crévéchamps** (again temporarily rejoining the main route). Continue through **Flavigny-sur-Moselle** and, soon after this village (where the road ahead leads onto a motorway), bear R over the Moselle. Immediately after crossing the river, and just before a canal bridge, turn L opposite **lock 45**. Follow a track down to the towpath to join the main route (see p70).

The main route continues from lock 33 on an asphalt track parallel with the towpath, past a series of fishing lakes R, to reach the end of the asphalt by the last lake. ◄ Fork L up a short stony incline onto a 4wd track on the towpath and continue for 250m to **Gripport** and lock 34. After another 500m, this track passes under a small green bridge then disappears completely. Turn R diagonally away from the canal across grass for 50m to pick up a good track that can be seen easily ahead. Continue past lock 35 on a track that becomes two narrow strips of asphalt, with grass in-between.

This is the point where Vosges département ends and the route enters Meurthe et Moselle.

Continue past **Bainville-aux-Miroirs** and lock 36 (10km, 257m) and at **lock 37** turn L over the canal to reach the D570 road just before Mangonville. Turn R and cycle on the road (no cycle lane), with the main and alternative routes temporarily becoming one to lead through **Mangonville** (11.5km, 252m) and reach the beginning of **Roville-devant-Bayon** (13km, 248m). Immediately past the 66km post, turn R off the D570, with the main and alternative routes splitting again, to cross over a millstream into Quartier du 4 Septembre. Keep ahead at two crossroads and then turn L along the west side of the canal before lock 38 on a stony 4wd track (do not cross the canal). At lock 39, pass a grain silo R and recross the canal to continue on the E side. Continue on a gravel 4wd track past **Neuviller-sur-Moselle** (16km, 243m) and at lock 40 take the R of two tracks parallel with the canal. Gravel at first, the track soon becomes asphalt and continues to **Crévéchamps** and **lock 41** (20km, 239m).

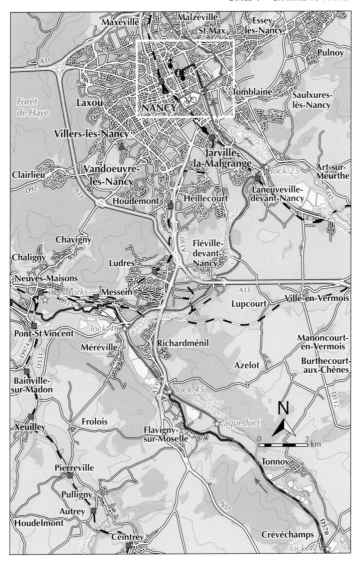

A boat crossing the aqueduct over the Moselle at Flavigny

Turn L over the canal then, after 100m, turn R onto the D570 (with the main and alternative routes again temporarily becoming one) and follow the road for 6km. ◄ At a distance of 350m past the 53km post, where the road starts rising to cross a canal bridge, fork R (with the main and alternative routes splitting again) onto an asphalt track parallel with the road. Turn R along the canal bank on a 500m section of muddy track through trees, which can be difficult when wet. Continue on an asphalt towpath over the **Flavigny-sur-Moselle aqueduct** across the Moselle and pass lock 43. After the lock, drop down R through a barrier onto a gravel road beside the canal and follow this as far as lock 44. Turn L over the canal and an overflow channel then turn immediately R to continue beside the canal, reaching **lock 45**. ◄

There is no cycle lane but there are regular km posts.

The alternative route for touring cycles fully rejoins the main route here.

Pass under a road bridge and bear L, away from the canal, to join a gravel track parallel to, but set back from, the canal. Pass under a motorway and continue with a series of lagoons L and **Richardménil** (31.5km, 224m) (accommodation, refreshments) on the other side of the canal. Fork L away from the canal to reach an asphalt road and follow this to reach a main road. Turn R on a cycle track beside this road to reach **lock 46** at **Méréville** (33km, 223m) (accommodation, refreshments). ▶

Cross the canal and turn R, heading back along the opposite side of lock 46. Bear L to reach a road bridge over the entrance to Canal de Jonction. Turn R over a bridge then turn immediately L alongside lock 5. Dogleg R then L over a millstream and join an asphalt towpath. This is well-signposted all the way to Nancy as part of the Boucles de la Moselle cycle route.

Continue past a series of five locks as the canal climbs over a low ridge, with **Ludres** (accommodation, refreshments) visible L across the canal. There are two locks numbered 1: the first marks the summit of the canal, which then continues to reach the second at the top of a flight of 10 locks descending into the Meurthe valley. At this second **lock 1**, the route first crosses the canal and then a busy main road at a roundabout in order to continue on the west bank, with **Fléville-devant-Nancy** across fields L. Recross to the east bank at lock 12, and fork L beside lock 13 in **Laneuveville-devant-Nancy** (44km, 203m) (accommodation, refreshments), following

This guide's main route leaves the Moselle here to continue via the architecturally stunning city of Nancy, rejoining the river at Frouard on the city's northern side. An alternative route, the Boucles de la Moselle, follows the Moselle via Toul (see Stage 4A; p75).

A flight of locks on the Canal de Jonction

71

the canal to pass under a road bridge. Where Canal de Jonction joins Canal de la Marne au Rhin, bear R then turn L above **lock 25** and turn sharply L again to drop down onto the towpath on the east bank of the canal.

Canal de la Marne au Rhin is one of the longest and most important links of the French inland waterways system. Linking the Paris Basin with the Rhine Valley, this 313km-long canal was constructed between 1838 and 1853 with 154 locks, four tunnels and an inclined plain. The canal is still used for freight traffic, although leisure use now predominates. Since 1973, when the Moselle was dammed and canalised, the canal has been split into two separate sections, with the part between Toul and Frouard abandoned in favour of using the river.

The impressive golden gates in Place Stanislas, Nancy

Continue with fields R and the suburbs of Nancy L beyond the Canal de la Marne au Rhin. Pass lock 26 at **Jarville-la-Malgrange** (refreshments) and go under the slip roads of a multi-level road junction.

The Art Nouveau museum of l'École de Nancy

After extensive car parks L, and just after a disused railway bridge, bear R (signed Tomblaine) up a ramp (to access the city centre, ignore this ramp; see p74) to reach the end of the stage at Rue Molitor in **Nancy** (47.5km, 196m) (accommodation, refreshments, tourist office, YH, cycle shop, station). ▶

Turn R on Rue Molitor to continue onto Stage 5, bypassing Nancy city centre (see p89).

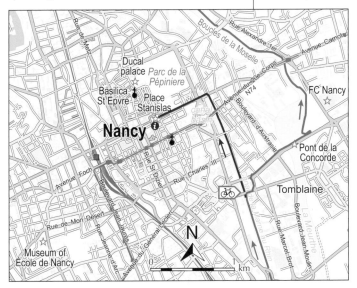

Extension to Nancy city centre

After passing the disued railway bridge, ignore the ramp up to Rue Molitor and instead keep ahead on the towpath for 1km, to reach the far end of a canal basin. Turn L here over a lifting bridge into Rue Sainte-Catherine, which leads to Place Stanislas.

NANCY

Nancy (pop. 410,000 (metropolitan area); 105,000 (city)) is on the river Meurthe above its confluence with the Moselle. It is the prefecture of Meurthe-et-Moselle département and former capital of the Duchy of Lorraine. The city grew up close to easily mined iron ore deposits at the lowest fording point over the Meurthe. During the French Revolution it was the scene of a major military mutiny, which was bloodily put down. Nancy remained French after the Franco–Prussian war (1871), with the population doubling by 1900 as the result of an influx of refugees who contributed to a period of economic prosperity and cultural activity. The most obvious manifestation of this was the 'École de Nancy', a group of architects, artists and designers brought together by glassmaker and furniture designer Émile Gallé, who worked in the Art Nouveau style of the late 19th and early 20th centuries. As a result, Nancy has a wide collection of Art Nouveau buildings and a museum of decorative arts.

The principal sight in the city centre is the 18th-century Place Stanislas, commissioned by and named after the last Duke of Lorraine and built over the ramparts of the medieval old city. Together with two neighbouring squares (Place de la Carriere and Place d'Alliance), all three of which are surrounded by stunning formal buildings, the area was declared a UNESCO World Heritage Site in 1983. Of particular note are the fountains, railings and Triumphal arch linking Place Stanislas and Place de la Carriere. North of the squares is the 15th-century old town, an area of narrow streets surrounding the Basilica St Epvre and the remains of the old ducal palace. To the south is the new town (17th century), built on a grid system with its own cathedral and market square.

STAGE 4A

Charmes to Toul

Start	Charmes, Place Henri Breton (284m)
Finish	Toul bridge (204m)
Distance	60.5km
Waymarking	None to Méréville, then Boucles de la Moselle to Toul

This stage is the first part of an alternative route following the Moselle through Toul, thus bypassing the main route via Nancy. The route description from Charmes to Méréville is covered in Stage 4. After Méréville, the river flows through an attractive gorge between wooded hills, closely followed by the well-surfaced and well-signposted Boucles de la Moselle cycle route. From Toul, the route continues as Stage 5A.

▸ Follow Stage 4 as far as **lock 46** in **Méréville** (33km, 223m) (accommodation, refreshments), then continue on the towpath on the west bank of the Canal des Vosges. Pass under a road bridge and bear L past **Messein** on the opposite bank. Continue under Messein bridge and after 300m turn L, passing allotments R. Follow the asphalt cycle track as it winds between lagoons, ignoring a plethora of gravel tracks to both the L and R. Bear L to circle around a large abandoned canal basin and follow a quiet road winding through waste ground between the Moselle L and canal R. Pass a steelworks on the opposite side of the canal and emerge onto a road with a cycle track, which is firstly on L but soon crosses to R. Follow this road as it bears R then L, passing Neuves-Maisons lock R. Continue under a railway bridge to reach a road bridge, with **Neuves-Maisons** (38km, 215m, 392**Mkm**) (accommodation, refreshments) opposite R and **Pont-St Vincent** L across the Moselle (refreshments).

See the maps in Stage 4; pp67 and 69.

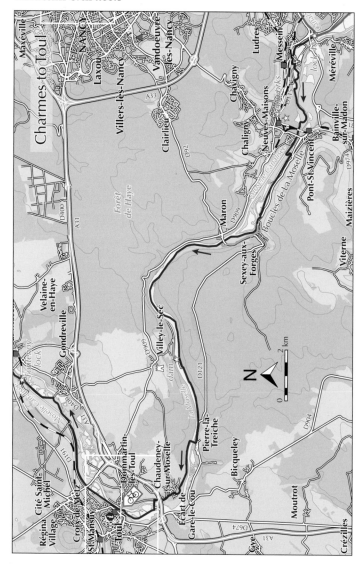

Charmes to Toul

Unloading scrap metal at Neuves-Maisons steelworks

Neuves-Maisons (pop. 6850) is an industrial town in the *Val de Fer* ('Iron Vale'). Iron ore was mined from 1874, with 700 miners working underground. However, low iron content (32 per cent compared with over 60 per cent iron in imported ore) led to the mine's closure in 1968. The steelworks, employing 4000 workers, continued in operation, using imported ore, until 1985. Since 1988 the site has been used to re-process scrap metal, employing 500 staff producing iron-reinforcing bars for concrete. The Moselle canalisée (constructed in the 1970s) allows large barges to reach Neuves-Maisons, which is 392km from Koblenz.

Do not cross the canal, but continue on the towpath for 850m. Follow a cycle track L between fields and climb up R to cross the Moselle. Turn R on a cycle track beside the river and continue past the hamlet of La Corvée to reach a road; turn R here into **Sexey-aux-Forges** (43km, 225m) (accommodation, refreshments).

Where this road bears L and ascends into the village, bear R on a gravel cycle track alongside the Moselle, passing below the village. ▶ This becomes a narrow

To avoid an unmade track, take the road through the village and, after 1km, where the road bears R over the river to Maron, fork L and bear R through a car park to regain the route along the river.

The brief alternative via Sexey-aux-Forges village rejoins the route here.

asphalt track, and where this has been undermined by the river, deviation is necessary onto a short muddy section through trees. Becoming gravel once more, the track passes a sports club L, goes under a bridge and reaches a car park L, with **Maron** on the opposite side of the river. ◀ Continue on an asphalt cycle track along the riverbank track for 7.5km to reach **Villey-le-Sec** lock (52km, 215m) (accommodation, refreshments, camping).

VILLEY-LE-SEC

Villey-le-Sec (pop. 350), on the hilltop opposite, sits inside one of the best-preserved late 19th-century fortifications in France, part of the Séré de Rivières defence line around Toul. After French defences proved ineffective in preventing Prussian invasion in 1870, a more sophisticated defence line was constructed to prevent further German incursions. This consisted of four heavily fortified military towns, each surrounded by a ring of outlying forts intended to prevent enemy artillery getting close enough to shell the main fortress. Villey-le-Sec was chosen for an outlying fort for Toul due to its position overlooking a bend in the Moselle.

It was originally planned to demolish the existing village and re-house its occupants. However, when this proved too expensive and time consuming, it was decided to build the fort around the village, the only place in France where this occured. Work started in 1875 and included barracks for 1300 troops and a narrow gauge railway system to connect the fort with outlying batteries. Soon after the first stage was completed, advances in weaponry dictated substantial additions, mostly in reinforced concrete. These were still unfinished when war broke out in 1914. Many of the lessons learned building the Séré de Rivières line were utilised for the Maginot line built after 1919. One of the oddest sights is a herd of Scottish Highland cattle, used to control the grass around the fort.

Immediately after the lock, emerge onto a road and turn L, following it as it bears R along the riverside to reach **Pierre-la-Treiche** (55km, 209m) (accommodation).

At the beginning of the village, fork R and turn R over the Moselle. Cross a disused railway line and turn L at a T-junction. Follow an undulating country road through woods to reach **Chaudeney-sur-Moselle** (58km, 212m)

Inside Villey-le-Sec fort

(refreshments). Enter the village on Rue de la Gare and turn R at a T-junction (Rue du Commandant Fiatte). After 100m, turn L into Rue Edmond Gérard and dogleg R then L over a staggered crossroads (with the parish church R) into Rue Léon Rampont. Bear L at a T-junction (Rue Émile Moselly), continuing under a motorway into Route de Toul.

Turn L at the first junction, following the D77 over the Moselle. Immediately after the bridge, where the road bears L, keep ahead on a track into woods to reach the canal. Turn R onto a cycle track along the canal bank, with lagoons R and the towers of Toul cathedral coming into view ahead. Opposite Toul lock, bear R away from the canal (signed Liverdun) past crazy golf L, and bear L alongside the Moselle to reach the end of the stage at Toul road bridge (60.5km, 204m, 371**Mkm**). ▶ To visit **Toul** (accommodation, refreshments, tourist office, cycle shop, station), double back sharply L then R to climb up onto the bridge. Cross the canal and turn R through fortifications into the town centre.

To begin Stage 5A, pass under the bridge and continue straight ahead (see p82).

Toul (pop. 17,000) became part of the Holy Roman Empire in 870, later becoming a free city within it, controlled by a powerful bishopric. The city was annexed by France in 1552 at the beginning of what was to become a steady French encroachment into Lorraine. This change was formally recognised by the HRE in the 1648 Treaty of Westphalia, when

Toul cathedral

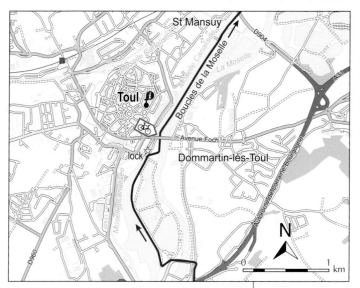

Toul became a part of the French province of Les Trois Évêchés (Three Bishoprics), along with Metz and Verdun.

The most striking features in Toul are the Vauban-designed fortifications that encircle and define the old town. Construction started in 1699 to a defiladed design of concentric five metre-high walls with moats in-between them. By the time of the Franco–Prussian war these defences were outdated, and in 1870 the city surrendered to the Prussians after only nine hours' resistance, when the defences proved ineffective against powerful artillery. Within the old town, the largest building is the Gothic cathedral, although it is in a poor state of preservation.

STAGE 5A

Toul to Pont-à-Mousson

Start	Toul bridge (204m)
Finish	Pont-à-Mousson bridge (181m)
Distance	49.5km
Waymarking	Boucles de la Moselle (intermittent) to Frouard, then none

This stage is a continuation of the alternative route that follows the Moselle, avoiding Nancy. From Toul to Frouard the Boucles de la Moselle cycle route is followed, although this section is neither continuous nor well-signposted, and some rough tracks and road sections are encountered. After Clévant lock the route rejoins the main route in Stage 5.

The medieval laundry house in Gondreville

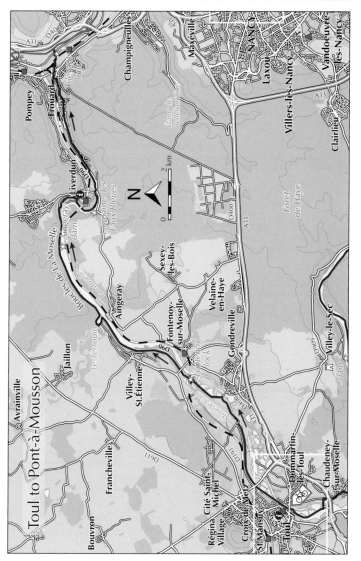

From under the road bridge in **Toul**, follow the cycle track along an embankment between the canal L and the Moselle R. Follow the canal bank for 4.5km, passing under a railway bridge and two road bridges. Soon after the second road bridge, dogleg R then L onto a country road parallel with the canal. Fork R away from the canal and continue to a T-junction. If you wish to visit **Gondreville** (5.5km, 198m) (accommodation, refreshments), turn R and cross the Moselle into the town; otherwise turn L at the junction to continue.

GONDREVILLE

Originally a small Roman settlement, Gondreville (pop. 2950), situated beside an important ford over the Moselle, is one of the oldest settlements in Lorraine. During the Dark Ages, control passed back and forth between Frankish kings, German dukes and the bishops of Toul. Taken by the Duke of Lorraine in 1154, the town was fortified, the castle enlarged and a bridge built. Apart from a short period under Burgundian rule (1475–1476), Gondreville remained in the hands of the Lorraine dukes for over 600 years, until 1766.

The town suffered greatly during the Thirty Years' War (1618–1648). Initially a struggle for power between catholic and protestant factions within the Holy Roman Empire, this conflict expanded to encompass much of Europe with an overall death toll of over eight million. On the front line between France (which temporarily annexed Lorraine) and the HRE, Gondreville and the surrounding region suffered greatly with armed conflict, famine and disease reducing the population by over 50 per cent.

The castle remained a ducal residence until 1715 and was demolished in 1751. A number of medieval buildings remain in the narrow streets of the old town, including the courthouse, tithe house and old laundry house. Nowadays, Gondreville is a rapidly expanding dormitory town for Nancy.

Head back to the canal bank. Cross the canal at the lock at **Fontenoy-sur-Moselle**, and turn sharply L then L again back under the bridge. Follow the cycle track along the towpath of an old, now filled-in, section of Canal de la Marne au Rhin and continue on the bank of the Moselle canalisée to pass **Villey-St Étienne** L (10km, 201m) (refreshments).

Villey-St Étienne rises above the filled-in former course of the Canal de la Marne au Rhin

Château Corbin, the Art Nouveau reconstruction of the former bishop's summer palace in Liverdun

Originally the site of a *fontaine-lavoir* (laundry-washing fountain), Le Terrouin, now a popular boating lake, was flooded when the Moselle was dammed and canalised, creating a lagoon.

Villey-St Étienne (pop. 1100) sits below another Séré de Rivières fort defending Toul. This was one of the last to be built, with construction starting in 1906 using entirely reinforced concrete and steel. Work was still going on when the First World War started in 1914 and it was never completed. From a much earlier age, a Merovingian dynasty (5th–8th century) graveyard with 115 graves was excavated in 1936.

Continue along the gravel towpath between the old canal course and the Moselle R, then fork R on a stony track past a series of three waste-water lagoons created within the old canal. At the entrance to a much bigger lagoon (**Le Terrouin**), bear L then R to cross a bridge and reach Pont de Fresnes (12.5km, 200m) (refreshments). ◀

Follow a country road circling clockwise around the lagoon to regain the riverbank and follow this for 4km to **Aingeray dam**. Continue on the road past the dam to reach the beginning of **Liverdun** (19.5km, 194m) (accommodation, refreshments, camping, tourist office, station). Fork R alongside the disused canal bed (Rue du Pisuy) and, where the canal disappears into an old tunnel, continue ahead through woods for 1km.

Alternative route via Liverdun
To visit **Liverdun**, continue ahead to pass below the castle L, and follow the road, bearing L through the centre of town (Rue de la Gare). Continue past the station, turn R at a crossroads (Rue Nicolas Noel) and follow the road towards the bridge, regaining the main route as it crosses over the river.

> **Liverdun** (pop. 6500), a medieval town and the former summer residence of the bishops of Toul, is perched on a rocky outcrop bordered on three sides by a U-shaped bend of the Moselle. For over a century (until 1973) it was surrounded by water, as the Canal de la Marne au Rhin passed north of the town in a tunnel under the hillside. This watercourse was abandoned when the Moselle was canalised.
>
> Ancient sights include Place de la Fontaine, which has niches containing medieval statues. Culturally the town came to prominence in the 1890s, when a number of Art Nouveau buildings, including the Domaine des Eaux Bleues beside the river and Château Corbin, which was built into the old bishops' castle, were commissioned by Antoine Corbin, principal patron of the École de Nancy design movement.

The main route turns sharply R off Rue du Pisuy (onto Ave Eugène Lerebourg) and follows the road curving L to the riverbank, continuing alongside it under a railway bridge. Pass a campsite and allotments L, with the Art Nouveau **Domaine des Eaux Bleues** across the river R. Just before Liverdun road bridge, turn L away from the river and then turn sharply R onto the bridge to cross the Moselle. ▶

The alternative route via Liverdun rejoins the main route here.

Once over the river, turn L and, after 20m, join a cycle track L of the main road. When this ends (after 1km), continue on the D90 main road (with no cycle lane) for 3.5km, passing Le Rond Chêne to reach **Frouard** (26.5km, 196m, 347**Mkm**) (accommodation, refreshments, cycle shop in Pompey, station).

Frouard (pop. 6650) is an industrial town at the confluence of the Moselle and the Meurthe. A medieval castle, built by the Duke of Lorraine in 1271, was destroyed in 1633 during the Thirty Years' War. The town started growing when first canal (1842) then railway (1852) connections opened up the area to industrial development. Iron ore mines, steelworks and flour mills were developed. In 1973, with canalisation of the Moselle, Frouard became an inland port serving Nancy. Asteroid 18635, discovered in 1998, was named 'Frouard' by its discoverer Alain Maury, who grew up in the town.

Pass a small square (Place Nationale) L, mostly used for car parking, and turn L downhill opposite a school (Collège Jean Lurçat) into Rue du Capitaine Marchal. Cross a bridge over the course of an abandoned canal and follow the road, bearing R (do not continue ahead over a railway bridge). Cross the D657 main road into Rue de l'Embanie and follow this road, winding under the railway and across the canal at **Clévant lock**. Turn R at a roundabout alongside the lock then turn immediately L onto a cycle track, which leads down past a recycling centre L to the banks of the Meurthe (27.5km, 188m). ◀ Turn L and follow the route description in Stage 5 (see p91) to continue on to the end of the stage at **Pont-à-Mousson** (49.5km, 181m).

To visit Nancy (accommodation, refreshments, tourist office, YH, cycle shop, station), turn R and follow Boucles de la Moselle beside the Meurthe for 13km.

STAGE 5

Nancy to Pont-à-Mousson

Start	Nancy, Rue Molitor (196m)
Finish	Pont-à-Mousson bridge (181m)
Distance	35km
Waymarking	Boucles de la Moselle to Frouard, then none

After leaving Nancy on the asphalt cycle tracks of the Boucles de la Moselle, following the Meurthe for 17km, the route follows the navigable Moselle canalisée north through a wide, mostly agricultural valley with scattered industrial locations. Although a route has been published for the stretch from Custines to Pont-à-Mousson, very little progress has been made in constructing the necessary infrastructure. As a result, a minor road is followed for 10km, followed by 8km on gravel or stony towpaths.

The Pont de la Concorde cycle and pedestrian bridge spans the Meurthe in Nancy

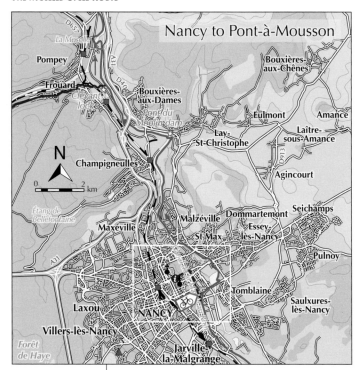

Nancy to Pont-à-Mousson

From the canal bridge on Rue Molitor in **Nancy**, head ENE on a cycle lane beside Rue de Tomblaine, part of a one-way system. Just before the first road junction turn L across the road onto a cycle track L of Rue des Sables. Cross the road at a T-junction onto the opposite side of Ave Charles Étienne Collignon and turn R on a cycle track that continues over two crossroads, then the impressive **Pont de la Concorde** dual-use cycle and pedestrian bridge over the Meurthe. Once over the river, drop down and turn sharply L then R along the riverbank, passing **FC Nancy football stadium** R. Follow the river for 7.5km as it winds past Nancy, passing a dam and red brick Grands Moulins (mills) opposite L, and **Malzéville**, where the cycle track doglegs L then R under the bridge (4km, 191m).

Continue past **Maxéville** and **Champigneulles** (station), both on the opposite bank L. At **Pont du Moulin dam** (8.5km), near **Lay-St-Christophe**, turn R away from the Meurthe then turn sharply L on a dual-use bridge above a weir. Turn R along the opposite bank, passing industrial units L and **Bouxières-aux-Dames** opposite R. Pass under a motorway bridge and immediately bear L, circling away from the river. When the track reaches the motorway again, turn R onto a cycle track beside a road and bear R back towards the Meurthe. Pass Frouard grain silos L and continue between the road L and the river below R to reach a junction (13km, 188m). ▸

The alternative Stage 5A from Toul rejoins the main route here.

Continue along the riverbank, with a factory L. Pass under a road bridge then circle L away from the river below offices. Pass under an old railway bridge then double back L on the cycle track across this bridge to cross the Moselle (signed Custines). Once over the bridge, bear

Large barges can use the Moselle canalisée

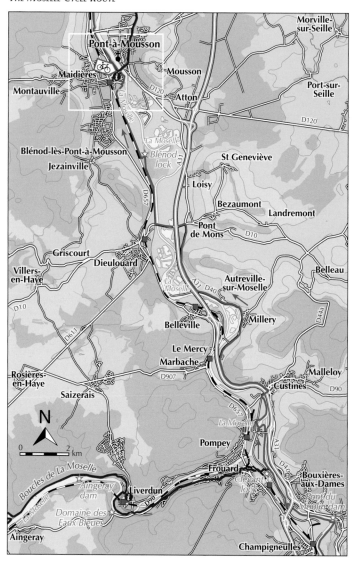

R at a crossroads before bearing R then L across railway tracks to reach a cycle track along the riverbank. Pass industrial units L and emerge onto a roundabout. Turn R back over the Moselle to reach **Custines** (17.5km, 190m) (accommodation, refreshments).

At a roundabout, turn L to follow the D40 out of the village. ▶ Continue for 10km through **Millery** (22.5km, 190m) and past **Autreville-sur-Moselle**. Follow the D40, bearing R away from the river, parallel to the motorway, and continue through woods and open country to reach the hamlet of **Pont de Mons** (27.5km, 182m).

At a crossroads 250m past the hamlet, turn L (D10), continuing over the motorway and the Moselle. Halfway over the river bridge, turn R onto a rough gravel towpath between the canal L and the Moselle R. ▶

Continue on the towpath, passing a power station R, to reach **Blénod lock**. Turn L over the canal and follow a road curving gently L then sharply R between a second lock L and an old factory R. Continue on a gravel track parallel to the canal past a large ironworks on

The D40 is a busy road with no cycle lane!

Continuing ahead over the canal reaches Dieulouard (accommodation, refreshments, station).

Place Duroc, the centre of Pont-à-Mousson

93

Premontrés abbey in Pont-à-Mousson

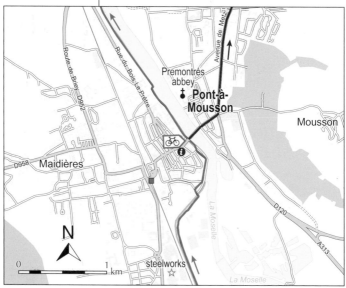

the opposite bank L. Where this track forks, take the L fork (closest to the canal) and pass under a pipe bridge. Emerge onto a road and follow it, bearing L over a bridge at Pont-à-Mousson lock.

Continue ahead over the millstream and turn immediately R along a road that becomes Quai Charles Françoise, to reach the end of the stage under the road bridge in **Pont-à-Mousson** (35.5km, 181m, 326**Mkm**) (accommodation, refreshments, tourist office, station). ▶

To reach Pont-à-Mousson centre, turn L immediately after the bridge into the market square and continue between houses into Place Duroc.

PONT-À-MOUSSON

Founded by the Comte de Bar (1239–1291), who built a castle on the left bank of the Moselle around which a walled town developed, Pont-à-Mousson (pop. 14,000) became part of Lorraine in 1431. In the centre of the town is the triangular-shaped Place Duroc, surrounded by arcaded houses. On the right bank, the University of Lorraine was founded in 1572 and soon gained an international reputation, drawing 2000 students from all over Europe. When the university relocated to Nancy (1768), the town declined in importance. All that remains is the Renaissance-style main courtyard, now named after Jesuit father Jacques Marquette, former student and professor, who discovered the source of the Mississippi in 1673. Also on the right bank, in a park beside the river, is the extensively restored 18th-century Premontrés Abbey. Nowadays the town is industrialised and is a major producer of iron pipes and halogen lighting.

One of Pont-à-Mousson's claims to fame is as the birthplace of Pierre Lallement (1843–1891), who, in 1862, built what many consider to have been the first bicycle. Failing to establish his invention in France, he moved to Connecticut and took out an American patent on his bicycle design in 1866. Commercial success again eluding him, he sold his patent and returned to France, only to find a bicycle craze in full swing – with models being made by Ernest Michaux, a man he had tried to interest in his original design. He returned to the US where, after working for the Pope company (who had bought his patent), he died in obscurity in 1891.

STAGE 6
Pont-à-Mousson to Metz

Start	Pont-à-Mousson bridge (181m)
Finish	Metz, Pont Éblé (164m)
Distance	33km
Waymarking	None to Novéant-sur-Moselle, then Véloroute Charles-le-Téméraire

Although a route has been published, cyclist-friendly infrastructure for the first part of this stage (through Meurthe et Moselle département) as far as Novéant-sur-Moselle has not yet been developed and some sections may be accessible only to mountain bikes and hybrids. An alternative road route exists following the D657 north from the eastern side of Pont-à-Mousson bridge to Corny-sur-Moselle. Once in Moselle département, a continuous, mostly asphalt cycle track proceeds through to Metz. Wooded hills close in on the west side of the valley as you approach Metz.

Alternative road route via the D657

Cross the Moselle in Pont-à-Mousson by Pont Gélot bridge and continue ahead on Rue Gambetta, passing St Martin's church L, to reach traffic lights. Turn L (Ave du Général Leclec D657) and follow this road, becoming Ave de Metz, out of town. ◀ Continue through open country, passing under the Paris–Strasbourg TGV high-speed railway line, into the village of **Champey-sur-Moselle** (6.5km, 175m) (accommodation, refreshments). Continue ahead through the village and on through open country past La Lobe hamlet to reach a road junction on the E side of Novéant bridge (14.5km). Rejoin the main route by forking L (signed Corny-sur-Moselle) immediately after passing this road junction (see p101).

The D657 is a busy road with no cycle lane.

From under the road bridge alongside the Moselle, the main route leaves **Pont-à-Mousson** by continuing NW.

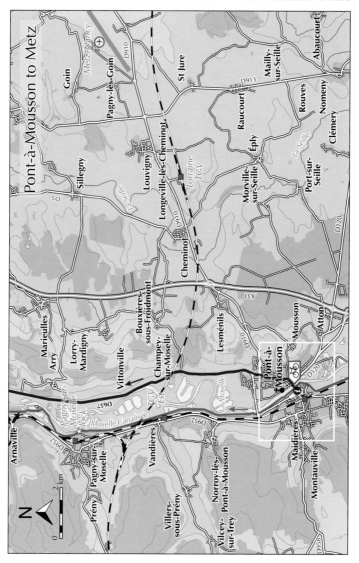

The TGV Est high-speed rail line from Paris to Strasbourg crosses the Moselle near Vandières

Where the road turns L away from the river, continue ahead on a gravel riverside track with first the university then Premontrés Abbey on the opposite bank. Zigzag R then L across an old lock and continue along a spit of land with water on both sides. Pass under a road bridge and zigzag R then L across another disused lock. Pass a bigger dam R and continue alongside the canal L. Pass **Norroy-lès-Pont-à-Mousson** L, an aggregates depot R, then **Vandières** L. Continue under a new railway bridge, which carries the TGV Est high-speed railway line from Paris to Strasbourg. Cross the canal at the next lock (**Pagny-sur-Moselle lock**), turn R (Quai du Canal) on the opposite bank and bear L on a dirt track alongside an old disused canal, passing a large factory L in **Pagny-sur-Moselle** (9.5km, 174m) (refreshments, station).

After passing a wooded area R and railway yards across the old canal L, turn R opposite an old lock L to follow a track through woods back to the main riverbank. After 1km fork L before woods and continue over a seasonal ford on a track between lagoons (with weekend cabins) to reach a crossing of tracks.

Alternative route for touring cycles

The section ahead is a rough unsurfaced track. To avoid this, turn L over the old canal on a short length of cobbles and bear R, parallel with the railway. Turn L under the railway and R at a T-junction onto the main road (D952). Pass under another railway bridge into **Arnaville** and turn R at a T-junction onto the D91. Continue along the main road, with the railway R, to reach **Novéant-sur-Moselle** (14.5km, 174m). Turn R under the railway line to rejoin the main route (see p101).

From the crossing of tracks, the main route continues ahead through woods on a narrow, muddy and rough track with the old canal L, and passes another disused lock. (Here the track improves slightly with old wooden sleepers, which gave purchase to horses' hooves, laid across the now wider track.) Do not despair, as after 850m you suddenly reach the border between départements: here a sign announces the Véloroute Charles-le-Téméraire and in the middle of nowhere a narrow muddy

The abrupt start of the Véloroute Charles-le-Téméraire, near Novéant-sur-Moselle

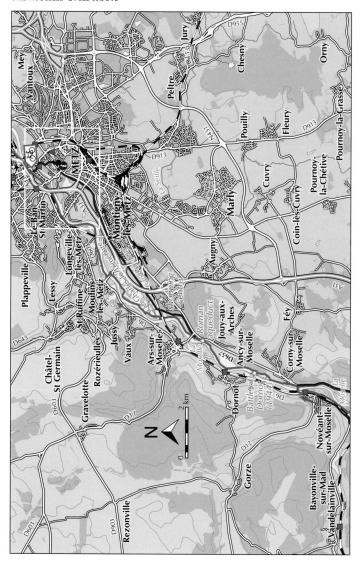

track instantly transforms into a 3m-wide asphalt cycle way. After 1km turn L over a small canal bridge then turn R along the other bank, with the railway line L, to soon reach a path junction L. ▶

Continue past the back of **Novéant-sur-Moselle** station (accommodation, refreshments, station) and turn L through a tunnel under the railway to reach the main road on its approach to Novéant bridge.

Turn L then R onto the main road by Novéant station and fork R uphill (D66), following the road over the river bridge. Turn L onto a cycle track just before a T-junction and fork immediately L (Rue de la Moselle) into **Corny-sur-Moselle** (16km, 174m) (refreshments, camping). ▶ Continue through the edge of the village and ahead onto an asphalt track to reach the riverbank. Pass a campsite R, turn R then L to pass around a small marina and bear L between lagoons. Continue past the site of the Second World War **Battle of Dornot** L, and turn L then R to regain the riverbank.

The US third army, which had swept across northern France from Normandy since D-day in June 1944, reached the Moselle in early September. As part of a plan to capture Metz, US infantry made a first crossing of the Moselle at **Dornot** on 8 September, and advanced to attack German fortified positions on hills east of the river. They were driven back by the firepower of German defenders, many of whom were drawn from the elite military school in Metz, and retreated to Horseshoe Wood, a small pocket by the river. Here, in a tough rear-guard action, over 500 US and 600 German troops died during four days of heavy fighting, before the Americans finally withdrew across the river. There is a memorial at the battle site.

Continue along the riverbank for 2.5km into woods, following a concrete track that skirts a series of small fishing lakes R to reach **Jouy-aux-Arches** (20.5km, 172m) (accommodation, refreshments).

The alternative route for touring cycles rejoins the main route here.

The alternative road route from the eastern side of Pont-à-Mousson bridge rejoins the main route here.

Memorial to the US soldiers who died in the Battle of Dornot (1944)

The Roman aqueduct at Jouy-Aux-Arches

Jouy-aux-Arches derives its name from the well-preserved ruins of a Roman aqueduct that straddles the village. This was part of a 22km-long channel bringing water to Roman Metz from a source in the hills on the western side of the Moselle. The channel crossed the river by means of this aqueduct, originally over 1km in length, which ran between Ars-sur-Moselle and Jouy-aux-Arches, where there was a settling tank to filter and clean the water. It then continued underground to Metz.

Continue on the riverbank track past the village, with a view of the **Roman aqueduct** R, to reach a small bridge L at the entrance to the Canal de Jouy. Here you are faced with a choice. The main route turns L over the bridge to follow a mostly good-condition asphalt track alongside the river as it passes just north of the centre of Metz (see p104). Alternatively, by continuing ahead for 9.5km alongside the canal on a gravel (and at some points narrow) track, you can directly reach the city centre.

Alternative route to Metz: the Canal de Jouy

Continue ahead on the gravel canal towpath. Pass under a road bridge and follow the canal, bearing L with a large out-of-town entertainment and **shopping centre** R (accommodation, refreshments, cycle shop). Turn L to cross the canal on a small bridge and R along the opposite bank. ▶

Pass under the railway, motorway and slip road bridges and continue for 7km along the towpath, passing the suburb of **Montigny-les-Metz** R. At Rue des Bateliers, turn L away from the canal for 50m then turn R on a road behind riverside properties and allotments. Bear R then L to regain the canal bank. Pass a winding place (a wider section of canal where boats can turn around) and **FC Metz football stadium** L, then go under two road bridges. Cross the canal at an old lock R and bear L then R on a dual-use track through the middle of Parc du Lac aux Cygnes through an avenue of trees, with **Plan d'Eau** lake L. Continue along the quayside under Moyen Pont bridge, to pass the large German **Temple Neuf church** at the tip of an island L. Just before the next bridge, turn R into a

You may be tempted to continue ahead on the R bank of the canal, as it is a wider, better-surfaced towpath, but ignore the temptation – the right bank is reserved for pedestrian-use only.

The Pompidou Centre for the arts in Metz

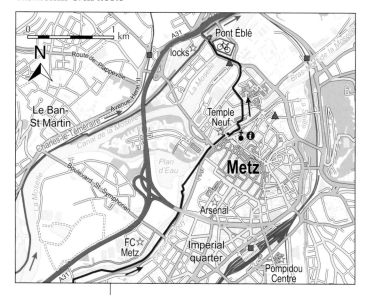

covered passage under Pont des Roches and emerge in
Rue des Roches near **St Étienne Cathedral** in the centre
of **Metz** (30.5km, 170m) (accommodation, refreshments,
YH, tourist office, cycle shop, station).

For the main route to Metz, turn L at the small bridge
at the entrance to the Canal de Jouy, following the track
over the bridge. Once across, turn R along the opposite
bank of the canal. Drop down under a road bridge and
follow an asphalt track as it bears L away from the canal
to follow the river and continue under a railway bridge.
Zigzag R then L away from the river and pass between
lagoons. (Ignore a turn R, which leads across the canal
to a shopping centre.) The asphalt ends by a house R
and a good-quality gravel track continues ahead, passing
between the Moselle L and a series of weekend homes.
Bear L at a junction and continue alongside the Étang
Marcel Bol lagoon R. Turn briefly away from the river and
turn L at a T-junction onto an asphalt road. Pass under a

road bridge and turn R on a cycle track that curves up and over the Moselle (26km, 168m).

Once over the bridge, at the edge of **Moulins-lès-Metz**, turn sharply R back down to the riverbank (refreshments) and turn L along the towpath. Pass a marina L, go under a red sandstone railway bridge and pass another lagoon L.

Continue between railway and river, with **Longeville-lès-Metz** L, then go under a road bridge, passing below **Le Ban-St Martin** L, and fork R by the ruins of an old bridge to avoid dropping down under the railway. At the next fork, bear R steeply up onto a footbridge and turn R then L across the Moselle canalisée. Continue along a narrow spit between river and canal past a dam R and go under a motorway bridge. Soon after passing under the motorway, you reach a fork 250m before a bridge. ▶ Fork L to pass under the bridge and continue along the riverbank as it heads north towards Thionville. Continue past a canal basin and Metz **locks** L, then pass under the next bridge (**Pont Éblé**) before turning sharply back R up and onto a cycle track on the R of the bridge (32.5km, 164m, 297**Mkm**), which marks the end of the stage.

For Metz, fork R and climb up onto the bridge. Turn R (Rue de Paris) and follow this road for 900m as it continues over two more bridges into the city centre.

Temple Neuf, Metz

METZ

Originating in the Bronze Age around 1000BC, Metz (pop. 430,000) was one of the principal settlements in Gaul. After capture by Julius Caesar it became an important Gallo–Roman city, with all the trappings of Roman civilisation including baths, aqueducts and a 25,000-seat amphitheatre. After Roman withdrawal it was the Merovingian capital and from the 10th century, along with the rest of Lorraine, it became part of the Germanic Holy Roman Empire. Metz was taken by the French in 1552, a position that was not officially recognised until the 1648 Treaty of Westphalia, when Metz became capital of the French province of the Three Bishoprics (Metz, Toul and Verdun). The rest of Lorraine passed into French hands in 1766, and Metz was reintegrated into Lorraine after the French Revolution (1789). Twice annexed by Germany (1871–1919 and 1940–1944), it has developed since the Second World War as the industrial capital of eastern France.

Architecturally, Metz has a wide variety of styles, most of which are grouped in distinct quarters. The oldest part is the Gothic (and former Roman) quarter on a small rise between the river Seille and an old arm of the Moselle. Here can be found St Étienne Cathedral, built of golden Jaumont limestone. The inside is a symphony in glass, with 6500m² of stained-glass windows including some modern examples by Marc Chagall. Also in this quarter are the town hall and other ancient buildings.

The German Imperial quarter, near the railway, contains buildings from the period between 1871 and 1919, including the massive railway station and the post office. The military quarter emphasises the strategic significance of the city to both German and French interests for many centuries. It contains the arsenal, the military governor's house and the esplanade gardens, formerly a parade ground. On an island between arms of the Moselle can be found the theatre and many of the administrative buildings for the region. In the south-west suburbs of the city is the impressive new Pompidou Centre for the arts, which has been built on an old industrial site. This is the first outstation of the Pompidou Centre in Paris, and the two will share exhibitions and performances.

Metz's most famous recent resident was European visionary Robert Schuman (1886–1963). Although born in Luxembourg, he moved to Metz and went on to become Prime Minister of France. While French Foreign Minister in 1950, he penned the Schuman Declaration, which proposed the creation of the European Coal and Steel Community. This was the forerunner of the European Union, and Schuman is thus widely regarded as the father of modern Europe.

STAGE 7
Metz to Thionville

Start	Metz, Pont Éblé (164m)
Finish	Thionville bridge (153m)
Distance	30km
Waymarking	Véloroute Charles-le-Téméraire

The area crossed on this stage was once the heartland of the French steel industry, but it is now a post-industrial landscape with very little active heavy industry visible close to the route. A surfaced cycle route, 'Véloroute Charles le Téméraire', mostly constructed along canal and river towpaths, connects the outskirts of Metz with the centre of Thionville. The going is completely flat.

Metz city centre to Pont Éblé

Regaining the main route, which passes north of **Metz** city centre, requires cycling 1.5km through city streets to reach Pont Éblé. Bearing slightly away from the river on Rue des Roches, continue through an archway and turn L to cross the river. Turn R (Place de la Préfecture, with the préfecture of Moselle département across the square L). Bear L (Rue du Pont Moreau) over a bridge and turn L at a T-junction (Rue des Bénédictins). At the next T-junction, turn R (Rue de Belle-Isle) on a cycle track L of the road beside a bus lane. Follow this, bearing L, and continue over the Moselle on Pont de Thionville into Rue Ste-Barbe, which leads to **Pont Éblé**, where a cycle track on the R of the bridge marks the start of Stage 7.

Stage 7 begins by crossing the Moselle canalisée on **Pont Éblé**, on a cycle track on the R of the bridge. Halfway across (do not continue over the motorway), turn immediately R on an asphalt cycle track down to the towpath. Pass under a combined road and rail bridge and follow

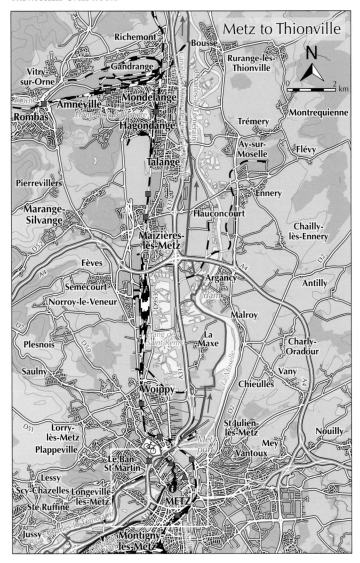

the cycle track beside the road (Rue de la Grange-aux-Dames), bearing L away from the river. Where the cycle lane ends, continue along the road (no cycle lane), crossing a railway line from **Metz port**, and fork L at the port entrance into Rue du Trou aux Serpents.

> The **Rue du Trou aux Serpents** gets its name from a well-known Metz legend concerning the Graoully, a dragon with a head bigger than its body and wide jaws with razor-sharp teeth. This dragon lived in the ruins of the Roman amphitheatre, along with a large number of serpents. When St Clément arrived to convert the city to Christianity, he captured the Graoully and threw it in the Seille, with the serpents diving in to follow it. The dragon was never seen again.

Pass between grain silos R and a malthouse L then continue past a 750m-long blue and yellow Ikea distribution centre R. ▸ Where the road turns L, beyond Ikea, turn R then immediately L towards a power station (signed La Maxe). Continue over a crossroads and, just before the power station entrance, turn R on an asphalt track between two small canals. Pass under a conveyor belt bringing coal from the quay and follow the track L.

Ignore cycle route signs indicating a R turn opposite Ikea along a muddy track.

Talange locks on Moselle canalisée

Dogleg L then R over a small canal, with nurseries R. At the next junction turn R (signed Argancy) and follow the riverside track for 3.5km, with **La Maxe** (accommodation, refreshments) visible across fields L. This track crosses a nature reserve, with hides in the bushes for viewing wildfowl on the lagoon. Bear L away from the river across a side stream and emerge through a barrier onto a quiet road (Rue d'Amelange). Turn R (signed Thionville) then R again over a canal bridge. Bear L and dogleg L then R over a stream and through a hamlet (refreshments) opposite **Argancy dam**.

Continue ahead, following the asphalt Véloroute Charles le Téméraire between a series of lagoons. Turn L and pass under a railway line. Shortly before reaching a motorway, bear L onto a cycle track beside the road, then cross this road and continue on the cycle track, now on the R. Bear R under the motorway, then fork L onto

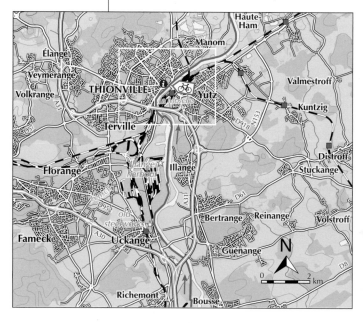

a cycle track beside the canal. Follow this along the R of the canal for 9.5km, passing a series of industrial settlements all set back from the canal and known collectively as the Sillon Mosellan, with a total population of 28,000: **Hauconcourt** R (13km, 159m) (accommodation, refreshments), **Talange** L (accommodation, refreshments), **Hagondange** L (station), **Mondelange** L (accommodation, refreshments), and **Richemont** L (19.5km, 157m) (refreshments), where the cycle route crosses to the L of the canal by a bridge just before the lock.

Pass a power station L and follow the towpath past the point where the canal and Moselle merge. Continue alongside the river under a motorway bridge to pass **Uckange** (23km, 155m) (station), where the preserved remains of an **old steelworks** can be seen between buildings L. Follow a wide bend of the river, passing the large but now underused **Illange Harbour** L, which once handled coal, iron ore and finished products from the steelworks of the Fensch valley.

Cross the canal by a new bridge at an old lock onto the right bank and continue along a spit of land between

The preserved remains of the old steelworks at Uckange

111

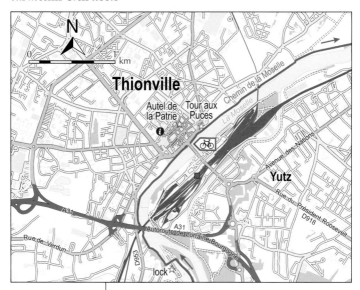

To reach Thionville city centre, fork L 100m before Thionville bridge and cross Quai Nicolas Crauser into the pedestrianised old town.

the canal L and Moselle R. Cross back to the left bank of the canal on a road over Thionville locks and immediately turn R on a cycle track alongside the river. Pass in quick succession under a motorway bridge, footbridge and railway bridge, with Thionville bridge ahead. ◄ Arrive on the quayside below the bridge in **Thionville** (30km, 153m, 268**Mkm**) (accommodation, refreshments, camping, tourist office, cycle shop, station).

THIONVILLE

Thionville (pop. 42,000) has been the centre of a great iron- and steel-producing area since the 18th century. Evidence exists of Roman iron ore mining, and iron production continued through medieval times.

In 1704 Jean Martin de Wendel bought a small ironworks in Hayange and from this developed a mining and steel empire with integrated steelworks and finishing mills spread along the Fensch and Orne valleys, southwest of Thionville, earning the city the title *la métropole du fer* ('iron city').

Industrial decline since the 1970s has killed off many of these operations, and much of the area has a post-industrial landscape of derelict industrial sites. The main operating steelworks is now a subsidiary of ArcelorMittal, the world's largest steel producer. Nowadays more of Thionville's residents commute to work in nearby Luxembourg than work in the steel industry.

Thionville's position close to the Franco–German border means the city has seen frequent changes in national control and a profusion of military construction. Prior to 1870 it was fortified with walls – originally designed by Vauban – to withstand attack from Germany in the north-east. Following capture by the Prussians, after a three-month siege in 1870, these fortifications were pulled down and replaced with a series of German hilltop forts surround-

Thionville's autel de la patrie

ing Thionville and Metz, which were designed to prevent any French attempt to recapture the area. After 1919, with the French back in control, the Maginot line east of the city was built to prevent further German incursions. This proved of limited use when, in 1940, the Germans circumvented these fortifications by invading France through Belgium. The hilltop forts, however, came back into use in 1944, when they were used by the German army to delay the US advance towards the Rhine.

Far from the industrial landscape south and west of the city, Thionville centre is an attractive maze of pedestrian streets in an area once bounded by the city walls. In Place Claude Arnoult is the only remaining *autel de la patrie* ('homeland altar') in France. Constructed throughout the country after the Revolution, these altars were used to celebrate the civil and revolutionary ceremonies that had replaced those of a religious nature, including the 'worship of reason'. The monument takes the form of an obelisk decorated with a radiating eye, which symbolises knowledge and the influence of enlightenment.

STAGE 8
Thionville to Remich

Start	Thionville bridge (153m)
Finish	Remich esplanade (142m)
Distance	39km
Waymarking	Chemin de la Moselle to Schengen, then Piste cyclable PC3

This stage crosses a rural border area known as *les trois frontiéres* ('the three borders'), which achieved fame in 1985 when the Schengen Agreement, abolishing national border controls within the EU, was signed on a boat moored in the Moselle at the three-country boundary point between France, Germany and Luxembourg. The valley is wide at first, but narrows approaching the border as the river enters a gorge through the Hünsruck Mountains, which it will follow all the way to Koblenz. Almost all of the cycling is on asphalt tracks.

The 12th-century Tour aux Puces in Thionville nowadays houses the local historical museum

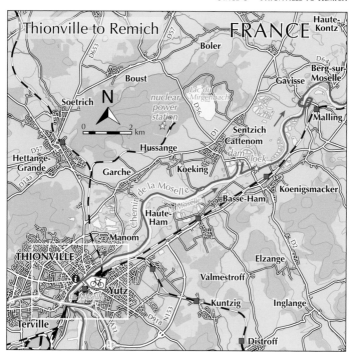

From under **Thionville** bridge, follow the cycle track NE alongside the river with **Tour aux Puces** L. Pass under a railway bridge and continue past **Manom** L. Where the road turns away from the river towards Garche, turn R over a stream on a cycle track that continues beside the river. Pass a nuclear power station with four reactors at **Cattenom** L, with **Basse-Ham** across the river R, a small village dominated by a large church. Pass a café beside an old ferry point (refreshments) and continue, bearing L to reach a dam over a loop in the river. Turn R over the dam (a very noisy ride over metal deck-plates) and turn R along the other side. Turn sharply L alongside the Moselle canalisée and turn R on a road over **Koenigsmacker** locks (11km, 149m) (accommodation, refreshments).

Basse-Ham church, on the opposite side of the river

Turn L along the right bank and, after 600m, turn L at a T-junction. Continue along the riverbank for 3.5km to pass under Malling bridge. After 400m, turn R to head slightly uphill and away from the river, then turn R again at a T-junction (Rue du Plan d'Eau). Continue over a crossroads in the centre of **Malling** (15.5km, 156m) (refreshments, camping).

Fork R at the next junction (D62) and cross the Moselle on Malling bridge. Follow the road as it bears R beyond the bridge and, after 300m, turn sharply R (signed Apach). Bear L on a cycle track alongside the river and pass below the villages of **Berg-sur-Moselle** L and **Rettel** across the river R. Cross a small stream and turn R onto a quiet road (D64) at a T-junction. Follow the road for 900m then bear R on a cycle track beside the river, passing below **Contz-les-Bains** to reach a bridge over the Moselle. Pass under the bridge and turn L, then L again, onto a road (D64) across the river. Turn L immediately after crossing the Moselle (do not cross the railway), then bear R. Turn L onto a cycle track beside the railway, pass a campsite L and continue between railway and river into **Sierck-les-Bains** (26.5km, 146m) (refreshments, camping, tourist office).

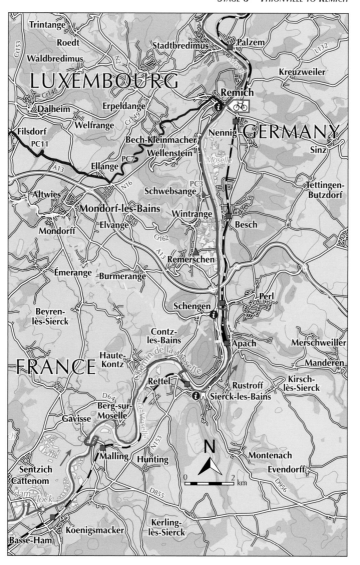

Sierck-les-Bains, the castle of the Dukes of Lorraine

Sierck-les-Bains (pop. 1750) is positioned below the walls and towers of a castle standing on a red sandstone bluff 50m above a tight bend of the Moselle. Originating in the 11th century as a residence of the Dukes of Lorraine, the current shape of the castle dates from the 15th century, with some 18th-century additions. When Sierck was integrated into France in 1661, the castle was decommissioned and its residential quarters dismantled. The defensive parts were partially restored between 1733 and 1752, with a renewed military role. Advances in artillery led to final military decommissioning in 1790, and in 1866 it became the property of the local community. It is now a popular tourist attraction, hosting a number of special events each summer (open March–November).

Just beyond the main part of the village, the cycle track ends. Turn R through a low and narrow bridge under the railway, then pass through a small car park and turn L onto a road between an avenue of trees. Beyond a small supermarket R, the road ends and becomes a cycle track alongside the railway L. The river now enters a gorge and the track passes beneath high retaining walls R with vineyards across the river L. Emerge onto a road past the old French border station of **Apach** L.

Bear L on a cycle track beside the railway yards. This reaches a road, where you turn sharply R uphill. Just before the top of the hill, turn L onto a cycle track (Chemin Robert Schuman) and immediately cross the Franco–German border. Follow this cycle track, parallel to the road R. Where the track turns L, bear R up an asphalt ramp to a roundabout and turn L downhill on the road. Continue across railway and river bridges to reach **Schengen**, in the country of Luxembourg (30.5km, 144m, 240**Mkm**) (accommodation, refreshments, tourist office, station in Perl).

The monument to the signing of the Schengen Agreement, with the Princesse Marie-Astrid in the background

Schengen (pop. 500), part of a three-country community along with Apach (France) and Perl (Germany), has a fame that spreads far beyond its local significance. In 1985 it was chosen as the

This fountain in Remich celebrates local wine production

location for the signing of a treaty between France, Germany and the Benelux nations that abolished immigration and border controls between them. This was signed on board the Princesse Marie-Astrid, a Moselle passenger boat moored at the conjunction point of the three countries. Subsequently, the treaty has been acceded to by many other European countries, creating a border-free area often referred to as the 'Schengen zone'. A monument made from three rusty steel girders, standing by the quayside in Schengen, commemorates this treaty, and a museum of Europe was opened in 2010 to mark the 25th anniversary of the signing.

Turn R immediately after crossing the bridges, passing the three countries monument on the riverbank beside the boat landing stage, and continue on a dual-use track beside the road. After 250m this bears away from the road and becomes an asphalt cycle track (PC3) along the riverbank. Pass under a motorway bridge and bear L to reach a road. Turn R on a cycle track beside this road and pass **Remerschen** L (refreshments, YH). Continue past a marina R, a campsite R and the village of **Bech-Kleinmacher** L to reach **Remich**. Bear R opposite car parks at the beginning of the town and continue on a dual-use riverside track that passes under Remich bridge (39km, 142m, 234**Mkm**) (accommodation, refreshments, camping, tourist office, cycle shop).

Remich (pop. 3000), the regional capital of southeast Luxembourg, is the centre of a wine-making community and a resort town. The Esplanade, with a French-style café-culture, attracts many German tourists.

STAGE 9
Remich to Trier

Start	Remich, Esplanade (142m)
Finish	Trier, Kaiser-Wilhelm-Brücke (130m)
Distance	43km
Waymarking	Piste cycleable PC3 to Wasserbillig, then Mosel-Radweg

Initially following the Luxembourg route du vin, with vineyards producing quality Riesling and sparkling Crémant on the slopes lining the valley, the route crosses the Sauer river into Germany and ends at the Roman city of Trier. Much of the route through Luxembourg is on cycle lanes marked on the main road following the river. In Germany, asphalt cycle tracks are followed. The going is completely flat.

From **Remich** Esplanade, continue N on the cycle track (PC3) between the main road (N10) L and the Mosel R to reach **Stadtbredimus** (3km) (accommodation, refreshments). Soon after passing the village, the route becomes a cycle lane to the R of the road, continuing through Hëttermillen as far as **Ehnen** (accommodation, refreshments, tourist office) (9.5km), where the cycle track reappears to the R of the road and leads into **Wormeldange** (11km, 140m) (accommodation, refreshments).

The cycle track ends before the bridge in Wormeldange, after which the route reverts to being a cycle lane. This continues, with extensive vineyards on both sides of the river, past the wine-producing village of **Ahn** (refreshments), before becoming a separate cycle track again shortly before **Machtum** (refreshments). This cycle track continues along the riverside into **Grevenmacher** (21km, 138m) (accommodation, refreshments, camping, tourist office).

Grevenmacher (pop. 3750) is an old town with the remains of medieval fortifications. Nowadays it is

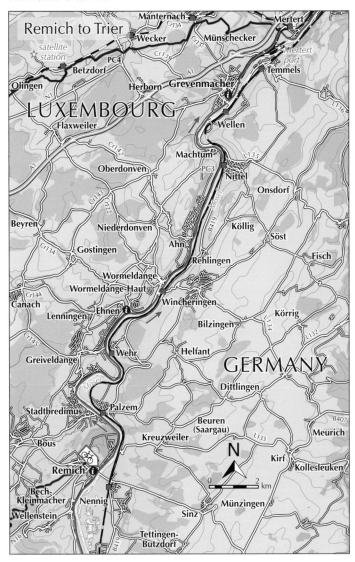

a wine-producing centre with the country's oldest wine cooperative and the Caves Bernard-Massard winery (founded in 1921), which is best known for its Crémant du Luxembourg: a sparkling wine made by the traditional Champagne method.

Cycle through the town on a cycle track that bears L away from the riverside just before the pleasure boat quays, to run alongside the main road. At a roundabout where the town ends, the cycle track bears R past a campsite R then turns sharply L to return to the roadside. After Grevenmacher the **Port de Mertert** (Luxembourg's only port) appears below R. The cycle track drops down R to pass under the port access road before continuing beside the road to reach the beginning of **Mertert**. ▶ Turn R on a cycle track under a railway. Dogleg L then R over

Grevenmacher's Bernard-Massard winery produces Crémant sparkling wine

The alternative Stage 9A via Luxembourg City rejoins the main route here.

123

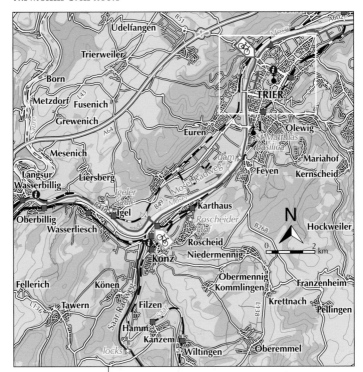

a stream and continue beside it to emerge on Rue de la Moselle on the riverside in Mertert (26.5km, 136m, 208**Mkm**) (accommodation, refreshments, camping, station).

Continue along the quayside on a cycle track beside the Mosel to pass the ferry ramp of the Wasserbillig–Oberbillig ferry in **Wasserbillig** (28.5km, 136m) (accommodation, refreshments, camping, tourist office, cycle shop, station).

At a distance of 100m before the point where the river Saure joins the Mosel, bear L up a red block track leading under the railway line and continue to reach the main road. Turn R and cross the bridge over the Saure

The Roman funerary monument in Igel reaches a significant height

To reach the centre of Igel with its Roman column turn L under the railway (signed Igel) and R at the main road.

into Germany. The cycle track continues through the village then drops R to run through fields beside the Mosel and pass below **Igel** (32km, 134m) (accommodation, refreshments, camping, station). ◄

The **area around Trier** was extensively settled by the Romans. At Igel there is a 23m-high Roman funerary monument (*säule*), erected in the third century by the Secundinius brothers, who were wealthy cloth merchants, in honour of their ancestors. It is highly carved with reliefs depicting the textile industry in Roman times and the passage of mortals to heaven. It survived the Middle Ages by being wrongly interpreted as showing the marriage of the Empress Helena, who was considered a saint by early Christians, to the Emperor Constantius Chlorus. Their son was the Emperor Constantine.

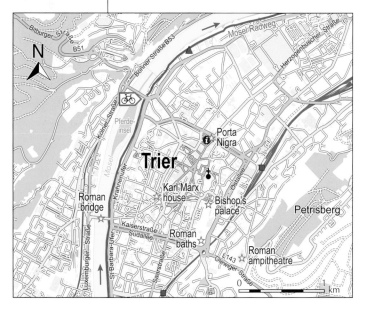

The much rebuilt Römerbrücke Roman bridge in Trier

Follow a quiet road along the riverbank that leads past a campsite L. Continue on a cycle track past the ruins of a red sandstone railway bridge L and past a point on the opposite bank where the Saar river joins the Mosel (**Mkm** 201). Cycle under **Konz** railway bridge. Turn L then L again over the bridge beside the railway line. ▶ Immediately after crossing the Mosel, turn L on a wide track dropping down to the yacht haven marina. Continue past the marina L and dogleg L then R to reach the riverbank. Continue along a riverside track, initially between the Mosel and a road, but eventually between the Mosel and the railway, to pass Trier locks and dam. Where the track splits, continue on the lower-level track and pass under a road bridge. (To visit **St Matthias Basilica** and see the cask in the crypt said to contain the apostle's bones, turn R at the bridge and cross the square to the basilica opposite.)

▶ Continue along the riverbank past two old manually operated cranes to reach the end of the stage at Kaiser-Wilhelm-Brücke, the main bridge of the city (43km, 130m, 192**Mkm**).

To follow Excursion 1 up the Saar valley, turn sharply L immediately after the bridge on an asphalt track descending directly to the riverbank and turn back L under the bridge (see p142).

Turn R at the next bridge (Römerbrücke) if you wish to visit the centre of Trier (accommodation, refreshments, YH, camping, tourist office, cycle shop, station).

TRIER

Trier (pop. 105,000) claims to be both the oldest city in Germany, having been founded by the Romans in 16BC, and the oldest seat of a Christian bishop north of the Alps. Its name is derived from the Treveri, a local Gallic tribe defeated by the Romans. It grew to house 70,000 inhabitants and was capital of Gallia Belgica and Roman prefecture of Gaul for 400 years. The most significant Roman buildings include the Porta Nigra ('black gate'), the best-preserved Roman city gate north of the Alps; Constantine's Basilica, a huge brick building that was the throne room of the Emperor Constantine and is now a protestant church; three Roman baths; an amphitheatre; and the second-century Römerbrücke ('Roman bridge'), which is still used by traffic, although much rebuilt. During Constantine's reign, the Roman Empire converted to Christianity and Constantine's mother Helena arranged for the holy tunic (the robe Jesus Christ was allegedly wearing when he died) and the bones of St Matthias (the 13th apostle, who replaced Judas after the Crucifixion) to be brought to Trier – where they remain, nowadays in the cathedral and St Matthias' Abbey respectively.

After the demise of the Romans and a period under Frankish rule, Trier experienced a long period of domination by the religious authorities. Widespread pilgrimages to visit the holy relics boosted the influence of the church and propelled the archbishop of Trier into a position of power as ruler over a state within the Holy Roman Empire extending from Lorraine to the Rhine. Two great spiritual buildings, the Romanesque cathedral and Gothic Liebfrauenkirche, as well as the rococo electoral palace, reflect the power of the church. Power diminished when the prince–archbishop moved to Koblenz and finally disappeared when the French swept away the electoral archbishopric in 1794. Of slightly more recent note, Karl Marx was born in Trier (1818) and his birthplace is now a museum documenting his life.

STAGE 9A

Remich to Trier via Luxembourg City

Start	Remich, Esplanade (142m)
Finish	Trier, Kaiser-Wilhelm-Brücke (130m)
Distance	85.5km
Waymarking	PC7, PC11, PC1, PC2, PC4, Mosel-Radweg

This stage is a longer alternative to Stage 9, heading up onto the rolling plateau of the Luxembourg countryside, to visit Luxembourg *Ville* ('City'), the capital of this small country. Return is via the rapidly growing new city of Kirchberg, home to many European institutions, then back across the plateau to regain the main route at Mertert, close to the German border. The stage follows a network of signposted, almost universally asphalt cycle routes (Pistes cyclable or PC), using cycle tracks (some along disused railway lines), country lanes and quiet country roads. The area's gently rolling hills mean this route has the most ups and downs of all stages in this guide.

From the Esplanade in **Remich**, pass under the bridge and turn immediately L up a small alleyway beside the bridge. Continue ahead uphill (Rue Enz, becoming Route de l'Europe) and turn L between two filling stations into Rue Nico Klopp (signed Scheierberg). Turn R at a round-about and immediately L (Jangelisbunn, piste cyclable PC7). Pass a cemetery R and at its end continue on a country lane winding through vineyards for 1.5km. Turn L and, after 50m, turn R on a road into Scheuerberg, with views of the rolling Luxembourg countryside R.

Continue through the hamlet onto a cycle track along the disused Jangelibahn railway line, winding first through vineyards and then into woods for 5km. Turn R at Ellange Gare (7.5km, 236m) (refreshments) onto a road (CR162) and, after 250m, fork L to bypass **Ellange**. Go ahead at a crossroads, ignoring a L turn to Mondorf, and continue through woods (now on PC11). Pass Bréim farm

129

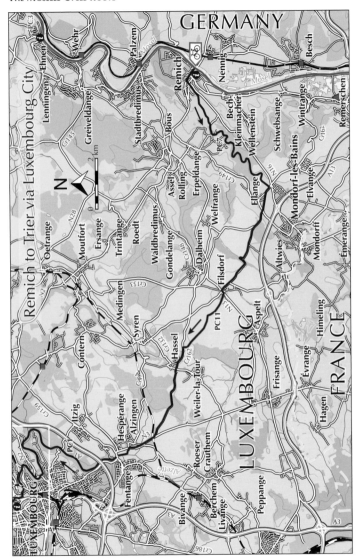

R and ascend around a hairpin bend L into more woods, then continue through fields to enter **Filsdorf** (13km, 292m) (refreshments) on Munneréfer-strooss.

LUXEMBOURGISH

While crossing Luxembourg you may come across the local language, Luxembourgish, which is spoken by about 320,000 people. It is a dialect derivative of High German, similar to that spoken in the neighbouring Eifel region of Germany, but with significant borrowing from French. Historically, it has tended to be a spoken rather than written language and those Luxembourgers who converse in Luxembourgish will usually correspond in French or German. Despite the small size of Luxembourg, the language has varied historically from district to district, leading to attempts in recent years to codify the vocabulary and grammar.

Luxembourg likes to regard itself as a truly multi-lingual nation. Unlike other such countries, such as Switzerland and Belgium, where language varies geographically, in Luxembourg language varies by function. Government proceedings are carried out in Luxembourgish but written laws are promulgated in French. Citizens can ask questions in Luxembourgish, French or German and expect a reply in their chosen language. In education, pre-school teaching is in Luxembourgish, but primary education is in German. In secondary school, language varies by subject and age, with German used in junior school and French the predominant language in senior school. Newspapers are mostly printed in German, but TV and radio are broadcast mainly in Luxembourgish. In restaurants, French is the norm, but in bars Luxembourgish is used. There is a class dimension too, with French more common in higher classes and German becoming more common lower down the social scale. When conversing with foreigners, the accepted custom of Luxembourgers is to reply in the language in which they were addressed, be it French, German or even Dutch or English.

Turn L in the middle of the village (Dräikantons-strooss) and, after 150m, turn R by a bus turning circle (Kaabesbierg) on a road that becomes a cycle track after the end of the village. Continue through fields for 2.5km over a rise then descend and turn L onto a road (CR162), with cycle lane R, that leads into **Hassel** (16.5km, 292m).

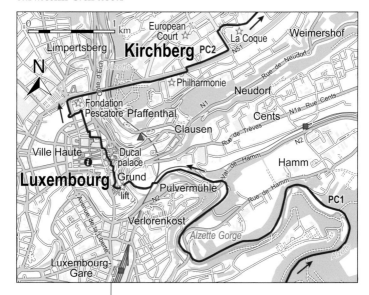

Continue through the village, following the road over a rise through woods, and descend to reach the outskirts of **Alzingen** (refreshments, camping). Turn R (Route de Thionville N3) on a road (cycle lane R) into the centre of the village, then turn L just after the church into Rue du Camping (signed camping). Pass the campsite R and, just before a bridge over the Alzette stream, turn R on a brick-block cycle track through a park. Fork L at a T-junction with a lake R, and continue parallel to the stream, passing an attractive wooden lifting bridge. Fork L onto a cycle track that drops down to follow the river under the main road in **Hesperange** (21.5km, 263m) (refreshments).

Continue ahead into Rue de l'Alzette (signed Luxembourg Grund), leading to a cycle track (PC1) that winds through the wooded Alzette Gorge, parallel to the river, for 6.5km. Emerge onto Rue Godchaux with houses R, and bear L to continue, following the Alzette through an archway under an old mill. Cross a main road and continue following the gorge into Rue de Pulvermühl. Cross another road ahead into Rue du Fort Dumoulin – ascending steeply for 70m – then, halfway up the hill, bear L onto a cycle track above a factory L. Continue, with a railway embankment rising R, then pass under the railway and go through an arch in the city walls. Continue into cobbled Bisserweg to reach **Grund** (31km, 249m) (refreshments), an area of bars and restaurants deep in the gorge below the centre of the city.

Turn L (Rue Munster) to cross the river. To reach the city centre, go straight ahead (signed Ville-Haute) down a tunnel lined with modern art, to arrive at a cycle and pedestrian **lift** that will take you and your cycle up through the cliffs to Ville-Haute in **Luxembourg City** (31km, 310m) (accommodation, refreshments, tourist office, cycle shop, station).

The wooden lifting bridge over the river Alzette in Hesperange

LUXEMBOURG CITY

Luxembourg City (pop. 94,000) is the capital of the Grand Duchy of Luxembourg. Occupied by a series of foreign powers, beginning with the Burgundians in the 15th century, the city was steadily fortified with defensive walls, bastions, casemates and batteries. The Spanish built 24km of tunnels and the defences were augmented by the French military engineer Vauban then were improved again under Austrian rule in the 18th century. During the French Revolutionary Wars, the city was only captured after a seven-month siege, leading to a French politician describing Luxembourg as 'the best fortress in the world, except Gibraltar'. Subsequently the city became known as the 'Gibraltar of the North'. These defences were dismantled as a consequence of an ultimately unsuccessful 1867 treaty that was aimed at defusing tension between the Prussians (who were occupying Luxembourg at the time) and the French. It took 16 years to demolish them.

The main part of the city, Ville-Haute, occupies a spectacular position atop a bluff overlooking the 70m-deep Alzette and Pétrusse gorges. Here can be found the Ducal Palace, Chamber of Deputies and courts of justice, together with major shopping and commercial streets. Grund, in the bottom of the gorge, was once a poor working class district but it has now been transformed into an area of bars and restaurants. A series of bridges span the gorges, including the Adolphe and Grand Duchess Charlotte bridges.

The lift brings you out in the judicial quarter. Turn R across a cobbled square surrounded by court buildings and pass under a covered walkway. Turn R (signed Circulaire Centre Ville-Haute) and bear L into Rue du St-Esprit, passing a viewpoint over the gorge R. Bear second L into Rue du Marche-aux-Herbes with the Chambre des Deputés R. Continue across the square ahead past the **Grand Ducal Palace** R, with an armed guard on sentry duty outside, and continue into Grand-Rue. Follow this as it bears L then turn R into Côte d'Eich. At Place du Théâtre, turn L around the far side of the square and continue into pedestrianised Rue Beaumont. Turn R (Rue des Capucins) then L (Rue Willy Goergen) and immediately turn R (Ave Pescatore), with the impressive **Fondation Pescatore** (a retirement home) ahead. Cross a main road and turn L at a mini-roundabout in front of the Fondation building onto a cycle track and follow this across a

main road into Parc de la Ville. Turn sharply R and head through the park to a road junction above Boulevard Robert Schuman.

The ruins of Luxembourg City's bastions

Turn R on a cycle track (PC2) parallel with the boulevard and cross the gorge on Pont Grande-Duchesse Charlotte. Continue alongside Ave John F Kennedy into **Kirchberg** (34.5km, 330m) (accommodation, refreshments, cycle shop).

> The new city of **Kirchberg** is situated on a plateau on the north-east side of the Alzette gorge, between Luxembourg City and the airport. This started life in the 1970s as home to a number of European institutions and now houses the European Court of Justice, Investment Bank, Court of Auditors, Secretariat of the Parliament and parts of the European Commission, many in innovative modern offices.
>
> Educationally, there is a European school and a new campus for the University of Luxembourg. On the commercial front, a number of banks have relocated their head offices to Kirchberg. There is also a large shopping mall and an international exhibition

The European Court of Justice, Kirchberg

centre. The Philharmonie is the country's national concert hall, while the Coque is a very distinctive indoor sports arena seating over 8000 spectators. Residential areas are being developed around the edge of the city and a tram system is planned.

Pass the **European Court of Justice** (a bronze building L) and the distinctive drum-shaped **Philharmonie** concert hall R. At traffic lights, 100m past the Philarmonie, cross the avenue using a red-painted cycle crossing. Continue along the other side past the Konrad Adenauer building L – this is used by the European Parliament. Turn L at traffic lights, go alongside Rue Érasme and turn R at a roundabout (Rue Léon Hengen). Bear R on a cycle track between a car park L and the **Coque** indoor arena R. Continue on the cycle track, bearing L opposite entrance number 1 of the Coque, passing between the University campus R and École Européenne L. Cross the road, continuing through Kirchberg Arboretum by following the left of two alternative tracks.

Cross the next road, with the Luxembourg offices of a number of large banks R, and, after 150m, turn L (Rue Alphonse Weicker) in front of a large shopping mall. Turn R at a T-junction on a cycle track beside Circuit de la Foire, passing Luxembourg's **messe** exhibition centre R. Opposite the end of the exhibition halls, cross the road L and continue on a cycle track on the opposite side. Follow the road bearing R, then fork L on a cycle track into **Grunwald** forest. Follow this for 4km, passing over a motorway junction, to arrive at **Senningerberg** (41.5km, 399m) (refreshments), which is located at the highest altitude of the route since before Remiremont on Stage 1.

Cross the main road, doglegging R then L ahead (Rue des Romains), and turn second L (Gromscheed) into a housing development. Fork L then follow Gromscheed as it bears R at a T-junction. Follow this road to its very end and turn sharply L on a cycle track descending into woods, with views of Hostert through trees below. Follow this track, crossing a road (Binnewee) and forking R over a small bridge at a path junction, to reach **Hostert** (44km, 346m) (refreshments).

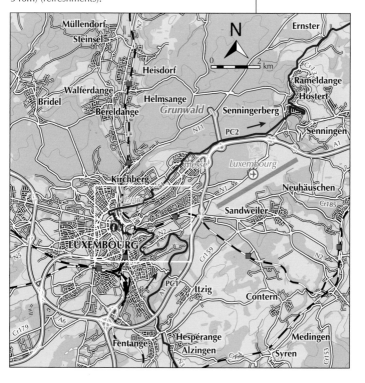

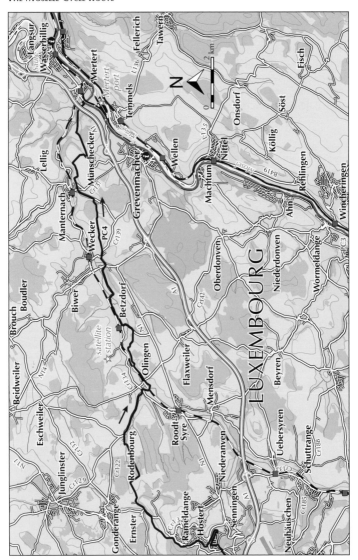

Hostert once housed a station on the 'Charly', a 46km narrow gauge railway between Luxembourg City and Echternach, which operated between 1904 and 1954. The station still exists and is now a restaurant called Charly's Gare. Parts of the cycle track both north and south of Hostert are along the trackbed of the disused railway.

Charly's Gare restaurant in Hostert, formerly the station building

Cross Rue de la Gare at a roundabout and continue through woods on Op der Bunn (becoming Rue Helenter). Fork L just before the 30kph restriction sign for **Rameldange**, cross a main road and continue winding through woods, passing above the village. Fork R out of the woods on a cycle track between fields. Turn L onto a road into **Ernster** (47km, 332m).

Turn R at a sharp bend before the centre of the village (Rue de Rodenbourg), leaving PC2 to follow PC4, and ascend gently past houses before descending on a country lane between fields. At a crossing of tracks, turn L (still PC4) into woods and continue on Rue d'Emster to a T-junction in **Rodenbourg**. Turn R (Rue de Wormeldange)

139

and follow this, bearing L into **Olingen** (52.5km, 233m) (refreshments).

Turn R at a T-junction and, where the main road bears R again, keep ahead on Rue de l'Église. Cross a railway and turn L on a quiet road parallel with the railway. Cross a main road and continue, at first parallel to the railway then bearing R through fields with a view of the **Astra satellite ground station** L, to reach a road. Turn L at a T-junction (Rue de la Grotte) and continue into **Betzdorf** (56.5km, 224m) (refreshments, station).

Although only a small village, **Betzdorf** (pop. 250) has two castles. The old castle in the village was bequeathed to a religious order, the Elizabeth sisters, and nowadays – with many modern additions – it houses the St Joseph Institute for disabled persons. The new castle (built in 1912), on a hillside overlooking Betzdorf, was used as the country home of Luxembourg's Grand Duke from 1953 to 1964. Since 1986 it has been the headquarters of Société Européenne de Satellites (SES), and in its grounds is the satellite ground station for Astra, Europe's first privately owned satellite operator. Using geostationary satellites, the company broadcasts to over 135 million European and North African households. The company is a leader in the development of digital, high-definition and 3D broadcasting systems. SES is the largest-value company whose shares are traded on the Luxembourg stock exchange.

Turn R (Rue de Wecker) in the village (CR134), with the buildings of the Elizabeth and St Joseph Institute on both sides. Continue parallel to the railway L. Bear R in Hagelsdorf over a bridge, then bear L to continue between fields. Cross the main road into Haaptstrooss and continue uphill through **Wecker** (59.5km, 229m) (refreshments, station).

Ignore turns to both sides then, at the end of the village, fork L on a cycle track between fields. Follow this for 2km, climbing through fields, and dogleg R then L to descend through trees to reach a road. Turn L and, after 800m, fork R beside a farm. ▸ At a hairpin bend, leave the road by continuing ahead on a cycle track between fields. Bear R uphill and, halfway up the hill, turn L. Fork L then turn R at a T-junction. Fork R at the top of the hill, with the Mosel valley now in view ahead.

The L fork leads to Manternach (refreshments, station).

Turn sharply L (signed Mertert) before **Münschecker** (avoiding the village) and descend through fields past a reconstruction of a Roman milestone R, and fork R with woods R. Continue downhill and pass under a motorway, then drop down to pass a factory L and reach a main road. Turn L on a gravel track beside this road to go past the factory entrance, and bear R beside a stream to pass under the road, where you rejoin the main route on Stage 9. Bear L under a railway, dogleg L then R over the stream and continue beside this stream to emerge on Rue de la Moselle on the riverside in **Mertert** (69km, 136m, 208**Mkm**) (accommodation, refreshments, camping, station). To continue on to the end of the stage, follow the route description from Mertert in Stage 9 (see p123) to reach Kaiser-Wilhelm-Brücke in Trier (85.5km, 130m, 192**Mkm**).

Astra satellite station in the grounds of Schloss Betzdorf

EXCURSION 1
Konz to Merzig: the Saar Valley

Start	Konz, Mosel railway bridge (131m)
Finish	Merzig station (173m)
Distance	49.5km
Waymarking	Saar-Radweg

The 246km-long Saar is the most significant of the Mosel's tributaries. It rises in the northern Vosges (France), runs through the German industrial area of Saarland, and then meanders through a gorge in the Hunsrück Mountains to join the Mosel at Konz, near Trier. This excursion gives a brief glimpse of the river, with a short ride upstream to Merzig. Almost the entire route is on waymarked asphalt cycle tracks through an attractive wooded gorge. Return by train, or cycle back on the other side of the river. The going is completely flat.

To visit Konz (accommodation, refreshments, camping, tourist office, cycle shop, station) turn L before the bridge, into the town centre.

From underneath **Konz** Mosel railway bridge, on the right bank of the Mosel, follow the cycle track upstream. Pass a campsite L and continue under a road bridge to join the start of the Saar riverbank. Pass under another railway bridge, then fork L away from the riverbank up to the next road bridge. ◀ Turn R across this bridge. On the opposite side of the river turn L across the road (signed Saarmündung) to reach the riverbank, and turn R beside the Saar.

> **Konz** (pop. 12,250) was an important Roman settlement (*Contoniacum*) and it housed the summer residence of Emperor Valentinian I (emperor AD364–375). A few remains of this palace can be found beside and under St Nikolas' church. More impressive is the open-air museum at Roscheider Hof, on a hillside above the town, where a 16th-century farm has been developed into a museum

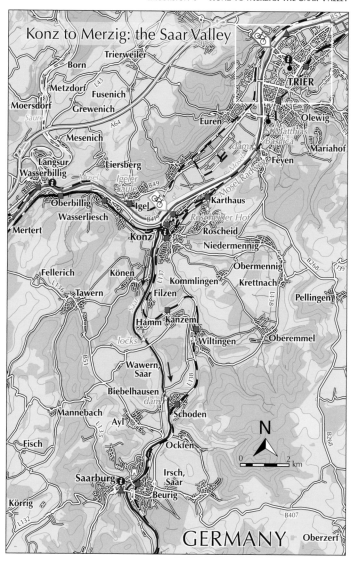

143

The village houses at Roscheider Hof open-air museum

of village life, with artisans' workshops, houses, a grocery shop and a schoolroom.

After 250m bear slightly away from the river around a little creek. After another 400m bear R then L onto a cycle track beside the road. At a roundabout turn L to head back to the riverside. Pass **Könen** R (refreshments, camping) and follow the cycle track for 3.5km, passing **Hamm** opposite, to reach **Kanzem locks**. ◀ Turn L, crossing the lock gate, and turn R along the opposite bank of the canal. At the end of the canal, turn L over Schoden dam, and turn L then R to continue along the towpath past **Schoden** (9km, 140m) (accommodation, refreshments, station).

From Kanzem locks to Schoden, the route follows a canal that bypasses a loop of the Saar past Kanzem village.

Continue south on the riverside cycle track, passing under a road bridge and behind a marina, to reach **Saarburg** bridge (13.5km, 144m, 12**SKm**) (accommodation, refreshments, YH, tourist office, station). ◀

To visit Saarburg, turn L 150m before the bridge, then R past the station and R again over the bridge. Pass through a short tunnel and turn L to the town centre.

The historical part of **Saarburg** (pop. 6700) is to be found on the west bank of the river. The first castle was built in 964 on Saarburg hill overlooking the

Saar. By the 14th century, a small town had grown up on the riverbank below the castle, at the confluence of the Saar and Leuk rivers. This grew into a medieval walled town, although only two towers remain following the mid-19th-century demolition of the fortifications.

Nowadays, Saarburg is the main centre of the Saar wine region, which produces high-quality Riesling. Principal tourist sights include a 20m waterfall bounded by old fishermen's and sailors' houses, which is located in the middle of town where the Leuk drops down to the Saar, and the ruins of Saarburg castle on the hill above town. The Mabilon bell foundry (1770s–2002) was the last foundry in Germany casting bronze bells. It is now a museum of bell making.

Pass under two road bridges and continue, following riverside cycle track to pass **Serrig** (18km, 145m) (accommodation, refreshments, station).

Saarburg castle

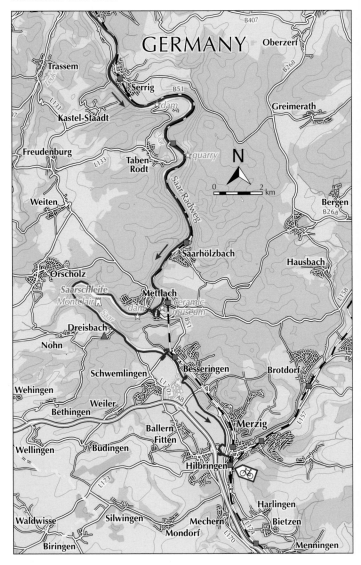

The route continues below sandstone quarries near Taben-Rodt

Sitting on a hillside overlooking Serrig (pop. 1600) is **Schloss Saarfels**, an early 20th-century castle built in an English medieval style (with wine cellars) as the centrepiece of a vineyard intended to produce champagne-style sparkling wine. Adolf Wagner, the son of a wealthy brewer, commissioned the castle and planted 75,000 vines on 12 hectares of hillside. After initial success, the estate suffered during the economic problems of the 1920s and went bankrupt in 1931. A series of owners followed, mostly other wineries, but the early success was never repeated and bankruptcy happened again in 1996. The castle is now privately owned but the vineyards are no longer cultivated.

At a distance of 2km beyond the village you reach Serrig **dam** and locks. Climb up L to reach a road over the locks, then turn L away from the river and immediately turn R onto a cycle track beside the main road. ▶ Continue into a narrow gorge, with wooded

The towpath carries on ahead but reaches a dead-end just beyond the locks.

147

hills on both sides of the Saar and road, and the railway and cycle track close beside the river. Pass under a road bridge, with Taben station L. As the river curves R through the gorge there are large red sandstone **quarries** terraced into the hillside L. Continue past **Taben-Rodt** on the opposite side of the river R. At the point where you enter Saarland state, the cycle track ends and becomes a red asphalt cycle lane that continues past **Saarhölzbach** (29km) and under a cable-stayed footbridge. Continue alongside the road to reach **Mettlach** (32.5km, 161m, 31**Skm**) (accommodation, refreshments, camping, tourist office, cycle shop, station).

Mettlach (pop. 12,500) houses the headquarters of Villeroy & Boch (and a number of its factories), and it is an important centre for the production of ceramics. Villeroy & Boch was founded in 1748 in Lorraine, then part of the Germanic Holy Roman Empire. Following the annexation of Lorraine by France and the vicissitudes of the French Revolution, the company moved first to Luxembourg in 1766 (where a factory operated until 2010) and then, in 1801, to Mettlach.

The sculpture garden in Mettlach

Although still owned by descendants of the founding families, it is no longer family-managed. In the buildings of an old Benedictine abbey overlooking the river, and adjacent to the company headquarters, is a ceramics museum and showroom displaying products from the 250-year history of the company. The museum also holds pictures by Anna and Eugene Boch (fourth generation descendants of the founder), who were friends and associates of Vincent van Gogh.

Other points of interest include the 1000 year-old *Alter Turm* ('old tower') in a small park next to the monastery, where there is also a collection of modern outdoor sculpture, and St Lutwinus' church,

A wedding reception tableau in Mettlach's Villery and Boch ceramic museum

decorated with ceramics and mosaics. Montclair castle stands high above a bend in the Saar, west of the town.

Continue on the cycle track beside the road, passing the **ceramic museum** L and Alter Turm in a small park L. Follow the cycle lane as it rises to Mettlach suspension bridge, and bear R across the Saar. After crossing the river, turn sharply L then bear R to follow a road along the riverbank past Mettlach **dam** and locks L. After the locks, the cycle track becomes a good gravel track. Steep cliffs R have catch fences to protect the track from falling rocks. The track follows the river around **Saarschleife**, a very tight 180° bend in a deep gorge, which is one of the most attractive stretches of the Saar.

Once around the bend, the track becomes a quiet asphalt road by an old ferry point (refreshments). Continue to the small village of **Dreisbach** (refreshments, YH) and turn L (cycle track L of road) on another quiet road beside the river (Nohnerstrasse). ▶ Where this bears away, turn L onto a cycle track past a small

Turn R and cycle 500m to reach Mettlach–Dreisbach youth hostel.

149

quay to reach Besseringen bridge. Pass under this bridge and turn R, parallel with the bridge approach, then turn sharply R onto the road and cross the river. Turn L (Ponterstrasse) and follow this street as it bears L. Fork R (ahead is a private road), then turn L downhill to reach the riverbank by Besseringen landing stage. Continue under the bridge and past **Besseringen** (43.5km, 168m) (refreshments).

At the end of the village, pass under the next bridge, then turn immediately L. Turn L then L again to recross the river on a dual-use cyclist- and pedestrian-only bridge. Once over the river, bear L and turn L to reach the riverbank. Turn R on a cycle track beside the river and pass under a bridge. Continue for 3km, then turn R and bear L around Merzig marina. Turn R at a T-junction and immediately turn L on a road with tennis courts R and a children's indoor play area L (refreshments). Turn L and follow the road past a modern brewery L. Pass under a road bridge and curve R, climbing to a road junction. Turn R on a cycle track beside a busy main road to cross the Saar for the last time. Continue ahead over a roundabout (Lothringer Strasse) and under a railway bridge. Turn R (Schankstrasse) and continue into Bahnhofstrasse to reach **Merzig** *hauptbahnhof* (main station) (49.5km, 173m, 45**Skm**) (accommodation, refreshments, camping, tourist office, cycle shop, station).

> **Merzig** (pop. 11,000) is best known as the centre of the Äppelkeschd, an apple-growing area, the products of which are used to make viez (a term for cider used in Saarland). An annual *Viezfest* is held in Merzig, usually on the second Saturday in October, when a viez queen is crowned. Notable buildings include the parish church of St Peter, the oldest Romanesque church in Saarland.

STAGE 10

Trier to Leiwen

Start	Trier, Kaiser-Wilhelm-Brücke (130m)
Finish	Leiwen riverside (119m)
Distance	32.5km
Waymarking	Mosel-Radweg

Here the route finally arrives at the Mosel gorge, following the right bank around wide meanders of the river and past the first of the vineyards. This is the start of the Roman wine road from Trier to Mainz, with numerous relics on show including villas, aqueducts and mileposts. The stage passes a series of quality wine-producing villages.

From Kaiser-Wilhelm-Brücke in **Trier**, follow the riverside cycle track on the right (east) bank of the Mosel. Fork R to stay above a series of cruise boat landing stages. Continue along the riverside, passing Trier youth hostel and then the perimeter wall of Nordbad swimming pool complex, both R. Fork L on a red-block path parallel with the river. Immediately after a big hotel R, turn R onto the entrance road of a supermarket and casino then, just before a round-about, turn L on a cycle track parallel with a motorway.

After 150m turn R under the motorway, then turn L (Loebstrasse) and first R (Rudolf-Diesel-Strasse). Continue through an industrial estate to reach a T-junction. Cross the road and turn L on a cycle lane R of the road (Metternichstrasse). Where this road bears L, turn R under a railway bridge, then turn R again and bear L beside a disused railway. Dogleg R then L over a railway crossing into Am Grüneberg and continue past a factory L into trees. Pass below an abandoned vineyard on the slopes R. Emerge onto a main road with a cycle lane R, which leads past a petrol station R into **Ruwer** (7km, 132m) (accommodation, refreshments).

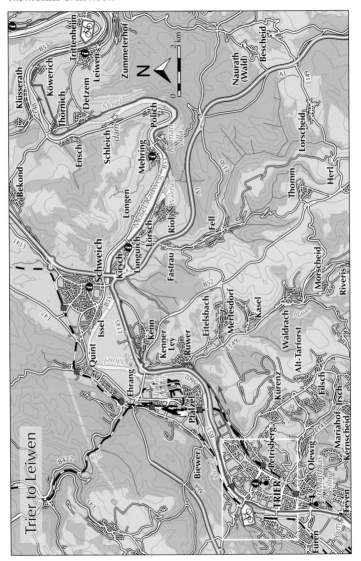

The fährtürme in Schweich

Ruwer is a small town at the head of a side valley through which flows the river Ruwer, another famous wine-growing area, mostly producing high-class wine from Riesling grapes. A 50km cycle track (Ruwer-Hochwald-Radweg) on the trackbed of an old railway follows the valley up into the Hunsrück Mountains. A short (9km each way) trip along the valley would enable you to visit Kasel (where the Kaselerhof inn dates from 1373), Waldrach (the principal town of the valley, with remains of a Roman aqueduct) and the ruins of Sommerau castle.

Continue across a small bridge over the river Ruwer and bear L uphill on Rheinstrasse, passing the church R. Follow Rheinstrasse as it bears L again and at the end of the village turn L across the road onto a cycle track between the road R and a motorway L. Continue under a motorway bridge then follow the cycle track, bearing R to reach a main road. Turn L alongside this road under another motorway bridge, dropping downhill and, after 150m, turn R across the road and fork R (Trierer

Strasse) into **Kenn** (9.5km, 136m) (accommodation, refreshments).

Turn second L (In der Ringebach) and then third R (Ringstrasse). Dogleg L then R across Bahnhofstrasse into Gewerbegebiet. Just before reaching a Coca-Cola depot, turn L at a crossroads. Continue, bearing R behind warehouses onto a cycle track parallel with the motorway L. After 1.7km, turn L onto a road to reach a motorway bridge. Turn R on a brick-block cycle track running along under the arches of the motorway viaduct, with the Mosel L. Just before a bridge over the Mosel, turn L across the road and bear R along the riverbank, passing under the bridge. ◀ Continue under another motorway bridge and bear L down to the riverbank. Pass the village of **Kirsch**, surrounded by orchards to reach, **Longuich** (15km, 126m) (accommodation, refreshments, tourist office).

Follow the cycle track under Longuich bridge (very low, you may need to duck!) and continue past **Riol** (accommodation, refreshments, camping), with vineyards now extending all the way down to the river. Pass **Waldsee** lagoon and a campsite (both R). Shortly after the

If you take the bridge across the river you reach Schweich (accommodation, refreshments, camping, tourist office, cycle shop, station).

Mehring's Roman villa rustica

campsite, the riverside track joins a road, and this is followed through woods to reach **Mehring** (19.5km, 128m) (accommodation, refreshments, camping, tourist office, cycle shop).

Mehring (pop. 2250), which spreads across both banks of the Mosel and is the fifth-largest wine-producing community in the gorge, was the site of an old Roman settlement. A second-century Roman *villa rustica* ('rural house'), which originally had 34 rooms, has been partly reconstructed in the village above the right bank. On the left bank promenade is a *fährtürme* ('ferry tower'), used for hailing the ferry that provided the only connection between the two parts of the village before the bridge was built.

Pass under Mehring bridge and continue ahead along the riverbank cycle track past a campsite R. Continue around a long sweeping bend to the L, with forest coming down to the river, to reach a road and follow this to Detzem dam and locks. Immediately after the locks, fork L off the road through trees on a cycle track back to the riverbank and follow this (Am Moselufer) past **Detzem** (25km, 120m) (accommodation, refreshments).

Detzem gets its name from a Roman milestone *ad Decimum Lapidem* ('the 10th milestone') that was found here. It indicated that Trier was 10 Roman miles away, along the Roman wine road. A reproduction of the milestone now stands in the centre of the village.

Continue along the cycle track, eventually moving about 100m away from the river. ▶ At the approach to the next bridge, bear gently R away from the bridge, then turn R away from the river (Moselstrasse) into **Thörnich** (27km, 122m) (accommodation, refreshments).

Continue through the village, crossing Hauptstrasse into Im Bungert and over two more crossroads. At the

The Roman milestone reproduction in Detzem

At this point the gorge has widened considerably and there is a large expanse of flat land on the inside of the river bend.

155

A typical patchwork of vineyards, above Klüsserath

This is the longest stretch through the vineyards on the whole trip.

third crossroads, noticeable because the roads cross at different angles and there is a small wine merchant ahead, turn L between vineyards. Continue on a cycle track through the vines for 1.6km, passing a builders' merchant's yard L and crossing straight over four crossroads. ◄ At the fifth crossroads, a Mosel-Radweg signpost to Köwerich directs you L back down towards the river, with Klüsserath visible on the opposite bank. At a T-junction turn R and follow the road, bearing L then R to continue into the pretty wine village of **Köwerich** (30km, 123m) (accommodation, refreshments).

Continue, winding through the village on Beethovenstrasse. Pass the church L and turn next L (Im Moselwinkel). Continue ahead at a staggered crossroads and pass under the main road. Turn R on a cycle track parallel with the road R to reach **Leiwen** (32.5km, 119m, 158**Mkm**) (accommodation, refreshments, tourist office).

Leiwen (pop. 1500), an attractive traditional village, is an important wine-producing centre. Its name comes from that of Livia, the wife of the Roman emperor Augustus, who had a summer villa here.

STAGE 11

Leiwen to Bernkastel-Kues

Start	Leiwen riverside (119m)
Finish	Bernkastel bridge (110m)
Distance	30km
Waymarking	Mosel-Radweg

The route continues along the right bank of the Mosel, following a series of tight meanders of the river. Some of Germany's greatest vineyards are passed, including those on the Goldötröpfchen slope at Piesport. This is a very popular cycling stage, in particular with many family groups. The cycling surface is excellent throughout.

Continue past **Leiwen** on the riverside cycle track to reach a road. Bear R ahead, crossing the road and continuing past a car park R away from the riverbank. Pass a

Leiwen's kneippanlage footbath

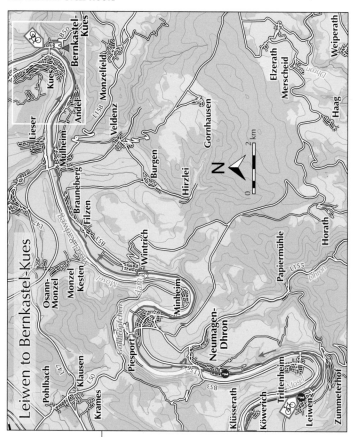

knieppanlage (a walk-through footbath for weary feet) L and bear L out of the village along the trackbed of a disused railway. Continue ahead through vines, to emerge on a raised alignment cut into the hillside just above the road L. Follow this around a long sweeping bend of the river with vineyards rising steeply R. Pass under **Trittenheim** bridge, flanked by ferry towers, and cross the main road R, then continue ahead on a cycle track just above the road L. This eventually drops down alongside the road and, after another 600m, turns R then L back into the vines. Pass a small chapel among the vines L, then drop down ahead to reach a road junction. Turn L then R onto a cycle track beside the main road and follow this into **Neumagen** (6km, 122m) (accommodation, refreshments, camping, tourist office, cycle shop).

> **Neumagen** (pop. 2200) is considered to be Germany's oldest wine-growing settlement. It was founded by the Romans as a fortified camp on the Trier–Mainz road. Archaeological evidence has shown that the Romans produced wine in the area and shipped it down the Mosel, with the most significant discovery being that of a carved stone wineship. The original is in the Landesmuseum in Trier, but a cast concrete copy is on display in the main street. A full-size wooden replica Roman galley has been constructed and, when not in use, it is moored in a small harbour on the riverbank. Below the church there is a garden named after the Roman poet Ausonius – who waxed lyrical about the Mosel. It has a statue of him.

Roman stone wineship found at Neumagen, now in Trier Landesmuseum

Neumagen's impressive reconstruction of a Roman galley

Continue on Römerstrasse through the town. Towards the end of the built-up area, turn L opposite a bus-turning circle onto Katharinenufer, dropping down towards the riverbank, and turn R (Moselstrasse) under a road bridge out of the village. After 700m, turn R under the road, following the Dhronbach stream L away from the river for 250m. Turn L over this stream and bear L back towards the road. Shortly before reaching the main road, turn sharply L to pass under a bridge, and bear R on a cycle track beside the road. After 350m, turn L then R between vines, then continue slightly above the river around a long sweeping bend R to reach **Piesport** (11km, 123m) (accommodation, refreshments, tourist office).

Piesport (pop. 500), a small village surrounded by 413 hectares of vineyard spread over both banks of the river, is the biggest wine-producing centre in the Mosel wine region. Settled by the Romans, who planted the first vineyards ('like an amphitheatre's rows' according to the Roman poet Ausonius), it housed the largest Roman wine pressing facility north of the Alps. Piesporter, as wine from the village is known, can vary greatly in quality. Inferior cheap 'export' wine, labelled as Piesporter Michelsberg and blended from Elbling and Muller Thurgau grapes, with sugar added to increase the alcohol level, has tended to give Piesporter a bad name. The highest-quality wine is produced from Riesling grapes, grown on the south-facing Goldtröpfchen slope on the left bank of the river.

At the beginning of the village, just past the cemetery L, turn L downhill to reach the riverbank. Turn R beside the river under Piesport bridge and continue away from the village on a riverside cycle track, with the famous **Goldtröpfchen** slope rising above the river on the opposite bank. Continue under Niederemmel bridge, passing Niederemmel village R and the rocky crags of the Moselloreley across the river, to emerge onto Moselstrasse. In 150m, after passing a parking place for campervans, fork R. ▶ Head uphill away from the river

This turn, which is designated as no entry for cars, but is permitted for cycles, is easily missed.

A view of Piesport, with Goldtröpfchen vineyard on the slopes above

and turn L on a cycle track beside the main road. Cross an approach road to Minheim Bridge and continue between the main road and the river, following a long sweeping L bend. Shortly before Wintrich **dam** and locks, fork L up a bridge slope and turn R over the road away from the river. Turn L (Moselweinstrasse) and continue into **Wintrich** (18km, 125m) (accommodation, refreshments, camping).

In the middle of the village, turn L (Moselstrasse) opposite the *rathaus* (town hall), where there is a fountain with a statue of a vineyard worker. Drop downhill, passing old village houses, continue over the main road on a bridge and turn R at a T-junction. Bear R past a caravan park L, and continue out of the village on a cycle track with vines R. After 1.5km, dogleg L then R and continue beside the river L. Just before **Filzen**, bear R away from the river, then turn immediately L at a junction of cycle tracks. After 400m, turn R away from the river again, heading steeply uphill for 50m, then turn sharply L back along the riverbank. Continue on Nussbaumallee, between the Mosel and the backs of houses fronting the main road, through **Brauneberg** (22.5km, 114m) (accommodation, refreshments, tourist office).

Bernkastel market square

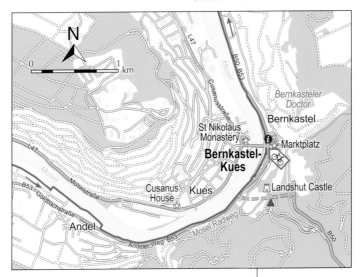

After the village, continue ahead on a cycle track through fields and then zigzag R twice to emerge beside a main road. Turn L beside the road and continue under Mülheim bridge into **Mülheim** (accommodation, refreshments, tourist office).

Immediately after the Weisser Bär ('Polar Bear') spa hotel, turn L and drop down to the riverbank. Turn R alongside the river for 250m, then bear R uphill and then L for 250m beside the road. ▶ Turn L then R away from the road and continue alongside vineyards parallel with the river to reach the beginning of Andel. Turn L at a T-junction and R at the next T-junction along the riverbank, passing **Andel** R (accommodation, refreshments, tourist office).

The R turn is easily missed.

Pass a launching ramp for a float plane on the riverbank and, at the end of the village, turn R uphill then L alongside the main road. As you approach Bernkastel, Landshut castle – on a hill R above the town – comes into view ahead. At the beginning of the town, the cycle track reaches a series of riverside car parks and continues ahead through these to reach **Bernkastel** bridge (30km,

110m, 129**Mkm**) (accommodation, refreshments, camping, YH, tourist office, cycle shop).

BERNKASTEL-KUES

The twin town of Bernkastel-Kues (pop. 6000) is the principal settlement of the middle part of the Mosel Gorge. The market square in the centre of Bernkastel is surrounded by half-timbered buildings, including the rathaus (1608) and a house built in 1583. In the middle of the square, the St Michael statue features the Archangel Michael bearing a gold sword. The ruins of Landshut castle stand above the vineyards that surround the town.

The best-known resident of Kues was the theologian, philosopher and later cardinal Nikolaus Cusanus (1401–1464), who took his name from the town. The St Nikolaus monastery, in the chapel of which his heart is buried, now houses a nursing home, wine museum and the Vinothek, a co-operative wine cellar where a wide range of the best local wines can be sampled and purchased. The most famous of these is the Bernkasteler Doctor, from the best vineyard above the town. Its name is derived from a 14th-century legend in which the Elector ('ruler') Beomund II, who lived in Landshut castle, became so seriously ill that doctors could not cure him. One of his knights gave him a glass of local wine and he quickly recovered. The wine became known as the 'Doctor'.

St Michael's church, Bernkastel, with Doctor vineyard behind

STAGE 12
Bernkastel-Kues to Zell

Start	Bernkastel bridge (110m)
Finish	Zell bridge (99m)
Distance	42km
Waymarking	Mosel-Radweg

The gorge still meanders tightly between vine- and forest-covered slopes. More attractive *wienorte* (wine towns) are passed as the route continues to follow the right bank of the river. After Trarbach the disused course of an old railway is used. The cycling is all on hard surfaces, except for a short gravel section through a nature reserve.

Continue north under **Bernkastel** bridge, with boat landing stages L. At the end of town bear R to join a cycle track beside the main road. This continues alongside the road to a point opposite the turn-off R for **Graach an der Mosel** (accommodation, refreshments, camping, tourist office). ▸ Turn L, leaving the road, and turn R along a riverside cycle track past a campsite R. Beyond the village, turn R away from the river – heading towards Der Josephshof – and turn L onto a cycle track alongside the main road. Follow this between road and river all the way to Zeltingen-Rachtig **dam** and locks, passing a large *sonnenuhr* ('**sundial**') set on the hillside above R. After the locks continue beside the road, past **Zeltingen** (6km, 109m) (accommodation, refreshments, camping, tourist office, cycle shop).

Zeltingen is a wine-producing village that holds the record for the price paid for a single bottle of Mosel wine, €2100 for a bottle of 2002 Trockenbeerauslesee from Zeltinger Sonnenuhr vineyard on the slope above the village. The village

To visit the pretty village of Graach, where the vines seem to rise from the end of every street, turn R across the main road and cycle through the village, re-joining the route beyond the village.

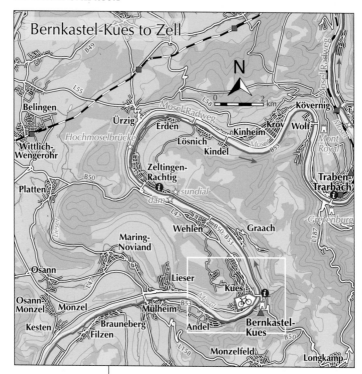

is also famous for a biennial operetta, Zeltinger Himmelreich, which is performed by more than 100 local amateur performers in the old marketplace.

Continue through a park between Zeltingen and the Mosel and on through a campsite. Pass under Zeltingen bridge and continue, moving R – closer to the road – to **Rachtig** (accommodation, refreshments). Opposite Rachtig boat landing stage L, turn R through an underpass and L (Gestadestrasse) in front of the Deutschherrenhof. Continue ahead, passing hotels and guesthouses R, and head out of the village on a cycle track beside the main road L. Just after Rachtig a new high-level motorway bridge (**Hochmoselbrücke**) is being constructed across the gorge. Dogleg R then L across a side road and continue past Ürzigermühle on Gänsfelderstrasse. Continue to **Erden** (accommodation, refreshments, camping), where another side road is crossed by a dogleg. Continue past the village on Am Moselufer, then bear L onto Brückenstrasse. Just before Lösnich, cross a spur road – built to connect with the Hochmoselbrücke – and, after 100m, turn L downhill and immediately R (Gestade) past **Lösnich** (12.5km, 108m) (accommodation, refreshments, camping, cycle shop).

Lösnich leads directly into **Kindel** (accommodation, refreshments), where the path drops down L onto a lower level of the riverbank. Pass under Kindel bridge and continue on the cycle track for 4.5km, following the river around a long bend L, through woods past **Kröv** on the opposite bank and past a campsite L to reach a road just before Wolf. Turn L (Uferstrasse), passing **Wolf** (accommodation, refreshments, camping, cycle shop).

Continue under Wolf bridge and, where the road bends R, go straight ahead on a cycle track parallel with

The sundial set among the Zeltinger Sonnenuhr vineyards

the river. Emerge onto a main road and continue along the cycle track beside this road R for 3km, to pass a Buddha museum R and reach a roundabout at the beginning of **Traben-Trarbach** (22km, 105m) (accommodation, refreshments, YH, tourist office, cycle shop, station).

Traben-Trarbach are twin towns joined by a road bridge built over the Mosel in 1898. Although this was blown up by retreating German forces in 1945, and replaced by a new bridge after the war, the quirky towers of the art noveau bridge house remain.

Two ruined fortifications stand above the towns, the Grevenburg above Trarbach (built in 1350; destroyed after a siege in 1734) and Mont Royal, an enormous Vauban-designed French fort above Traben (dating from 1687). The latter was built to house 22,000 soldiers and 3000 horses, but was only used for 11 years due to French withdrawal in 1698.

The Art Noveau bridge tower in Traben-Trarbach

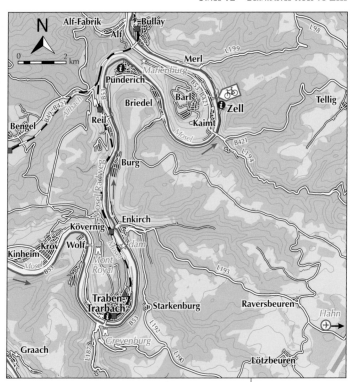

The cycle track bears L at the roundabout, then turns immediately R through a riverside car park and gardens to pass under Traben bridge. Continue on a cycle track alongside the main road for 4km to reach Enkirch **dam** and locks. Bear slightly L, behind a wall, and continue parallel with the road past a children's play area to reach the turn-off for **Enkirch** (27km, 101m) (accommodation, refreshments, tourist office).

> **Enkirch** (pop. 1600) has so many half-timbered houses, built between the 15th and 18th centuries, that the village is known as the *Schatzkammer*

Rheinischen Fachwerkhaues ('treasury of Rhenish timber-framing'). It was originally a walled town with seven gates, and a few remnants of the fortifications remain. Other interesting historical artefacts include a number of carved artisans' signs and the *Drilles im Spilles*, a revolving cage for punishing prisoners.

Bear L away from the main road, across a small bridge, then bear R past a camper van park L and turn L on a cycle track beside the main road. Continue to the end of the village and follow the cycle track, turning L away from the road and bearing R to run parallel with the Mosel, with allotments then vineyards R. Continue for 1.5km, passing a marker stone L showing the point where the track crosses 50°N, to reach a fork about 300m before the beginning of Burg. Fork R to reach the main road and turn L on a cycle track beside the road. Continue to reach **Burg** (30km, 105m) (accommodation, refreshments, tourist office).

Continue past the village alongside the main road and pass under **Reil** bridge then, 350m beyond the bridge, dogleg L then R to join a country lane. Follow this, zigzagging L then R between the vines, and turn L at a crossroads towards a campsite. Turn R just before the campsite entrance and follow a track between the river L and vineyards R for 2km, curving around a R bend of the river to reach **Pünderich** (35km, 101m) (accommodation, refreshments, camping, tourist office).

Pünderich (pop. 900) has a large number of old half-timbered buildings, of particular note being the much-photographed old rathaus (1548) and old *fährhaus* ('ferry house') (1621), both in Marienburgerstrasse. The town hall bears an inscription advising you not to enter unless you can hold your wine.

Opposite Pünderich is Petersberg hill, covered by vineyards and with the Marienburg (a former Augustinian monastery) on its summit. The

The fährhaus *and* rathaus *in Pünderich*

monastery was dissolved in 1515, when Marienburg became a fortress. It now serves as a youth education centre. Its position, right on the neck of the Zeller Hamm meander, gives it views down into two different reaches of the Mosel gorge.

Continue through the village, passing the half-timbered rathaus and fährhaus R, opposite the ferry landing stage and a car park L. In the middle of a campsite, zig-zag L then R to reach the riverbank and continue along the riverside cycle track on the trackbed of a disused railway for 2.5km to **Briedel** (accommodation, refreshments, tourist office).

Continue below Briedel past a car ferry ramp and on along the riverbank beyond the village. Enter woods where the forested slopes of the gorge come directly down to the river. For two short stretches through a nature reserve the track becomes gravel (good surface). After a short section beside the main road, fork L downhill on a gravel track under **Kaimt** bridge. Beyond the bridge, continue along the riverbank (now brick-block), with the first buildings of Zell R, to a point opposite a small roundabout by an attractive half-timbered building R, at the entrance to Balduinstrasse. ▶ Turn R across the road and turn L along the riverside promenade (Brandenburg). Continue to reach **Zell** pedestrian and cycle bridge

Balduinstrasse was formerly the main street through Zell. It has been pedestrianised and cannot be used by cyclists.

Pedestrianised Balduinstrasse was formerly the main street through Zell

Statue of the Schwarze Katz in Zell

(42km, 99m, 87**Mkm**) (accommodation, refreshments, camping, tourist office, cycle shop).

Zell (pop. 4300) is an old medieval town, the walls of which were constructed in 1229 and demolished during an 18th-century French occupation. Two towers standing in the vineyards, one round and one square, are remnants of these fortifications.

Zell is the second-largest wine-producing town in the Mosel valley (after Piesport). The most famous wine is that of the Zeller Schwarze Katz ('black cat') vineyard, which got its name when a group of wine merchants from Aachen were visiting the town to purchase wine in bulk. They were undecided about which wine to buy until a black cat jumped on top of one of the barrels, snarling and spitting and with its back arched. Convinced that the cat was protecting the best wine, they bought the barrel and took it back to Aachen. Within a short time they were back buying more. To this day the black cat appears on Zell's best wine and a statue of a snarling cat graces the town centre.

STAGE 13
Zell to Cochem

Start	Zell bridge (99m)
Finish	Cochem bridge (85m)
Distance	36km
Waymarking	Mosel-Radweg

This is the steepest part of the gorge, known below Bremm as the Cochemer Krampen, where the gradients of the sides reach up to 75 per cent. Vines are tended and grapes harvested by means of aerial cableways and steep rail tracks up the gorge side. The cycling is generally flat, with one short steep climb above the river.

Continue north under **Zell** pedestrian and cycle bridge, bearing L on a cycle route past a series of riverside car parks. At the end of these car parks, follow the cycle track alongside the river to pass **Merl**.

> **Merl** is a small village of wineries, half-timbered houses and two churches, one dating from 1490. The wine industry is omnipresent, with the impedimenta of wine production everywhere, including half barrels and wine presses used as street furniture.

Continue along the riverside, with a view of Marienburg (which was visible from the other side on Stage 12) on top of the hillside across the river L. Just before the village of Bullay, dogleg R then L to pass under its combined road and rail bridge. Bear L, continuing along the riverside (ignoring signs for Bullay Gare) past a campsite and then sports fields R to reach a turn-off for the centre of **Bullay** (5km, 96m) (accommodation, refreshments, camping, tourist office, station).

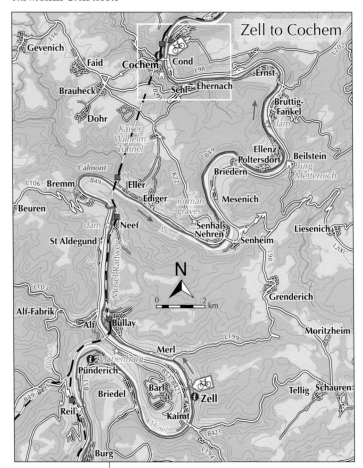

Apart from having Germany's only double-deck road and rail bridge (opened in 1878) – with trains above and vehicles below – **Bullay** is a wine-producing village; its main wine is Bullayer Brautrock.

This wine gets its name from the legend of the son of an impoverished count, whose father had

Bullay is home to Germany's only dual road and rail bridge

dissipated the family fortune on a lavish lifestyle, who wished to marry the daughter of a wealthy knight. In those times it was customary for the groom's father to pay for a wedding, but the count could not afford to do this. The knight advanced him the money against the security of a vineyard called Brautrock ('bridal gown'), but stipulated that the proceeds from all wine sold would belong to his daughter in case his son-in-law turned out to be as imprudent with money as his father. A statue of a naked bride holding her wedding gown is in the town square.

Continue past Bullay along the riverside, with pretty gardens and houses set back R. Soon after the end of the village, bear R uphill and cross the main road. ▶ Continue uphill under a railway bridge. Turn L, continuing to climb for 100m, then drop down again beside the railway line, where the track becomes gravel. Continue undulating beside the railway for 2km, then turn L under the railway to emerge suddenly on the main road. Turn R on this road (narrow, with no cycle lane), passing **St Aldegund** on the other side of the river L. Pass Neef **dam** and locks and

To avoid a 2km section on rough gravel, turn L and cycle along the main road (which is narrow, with no cycle lane) as far as Neef locks.

175

*Bullayer Blautrock
statue in Bullay*

continue on the road into **Neef** (9km, 95m) (accommodation, refreshments, camping, tourist office, station).

In the middle of the village, follow the main road (Moseluferstrasse), bearing R away from the river, then bear L across Neef bridge to reach the L bank of the Mosel for the first time since Konz. Drop down R to the main road and cross straight over at a busy T-junction onto a cycle track opposite. Bear L and follow this track parallel to the river, with allotments L. Rejoin the main road and continue on a cycle track on the R of the road through **Bremm** (accommodation, refreshments, tourist office).

As the river rounds the bend from Bremm, the slopes and cliffs rising L are the steepest part of the entire gorge. The Calmont **klettersteig** ('aided path') starts from the church just above the centre of the village and runs for 3km, crossing the slopes of the steepest vineyard in Europe. En route there are six ladders, 22 stirrups, 16 spikes and about 100 sections of cable. The route takes between two and three hours to complete, and ends at Ediger-Eller station. Proper footwear is essential.

Continue beside the road, following the river as it bends sharply R below the Calmont slopes, with little railway lines running up the hillside L to enable the vines to be tended. Bear R, following the cycle track away from the road, and pass under Eller railway bridge. Continue past **Eller** (accommodation, refreshments, station) and **Ediger** (15km, 91m) (accommodation, refreshments, camping, tourist office), staying close to the river.

The railway that crosses the river before Eller is the **Moselbahn**, part of the Cannonbahn, opened in 1879 to link Berlin with Metz in the territory captured during the Franco–Prussian War. It includes a number of major civil engineering works, including the Kaiser Wilhelm tunnel between Cochem and Eller (4205m), which was the longest in Germany when built.

During the First World War, this single-track tunnel became a bottleneck on a supply route to the Western Front. A new route along the right bank between Karden and Bullay was started in 1916, but was unfinished when the war ended and was abandoned, unused, in 1923. During the Second World War a tunnel on the abandoned route was used as a concentration camp, with 13,000 prisoners providing slave labour for an underground factory producing ignition systems for military vehicles. Work to provide a second tunnel finally began in 2010 and will be finished in 2016, 100 years after the original scheme was started.

Pass a campsite L and continue along the riverbank, passing **Nehren** (accommodation, camping), which sits L behind a backwater (Nehren Laach). Continue through a campsite and pass under a road bridge to reach **Senhals** (19.5km, 92m) (accommodation, refreshments, camping, tourist office).

In the vineyards 150m above Nehren, but reached from Senhals (2.4km), are **Roman burial chambers** from the third and fourth centuries. The wall paintings inside are original and the best-preserved of their kind north of the Alps. The upper parts of the monuments are reconstructions.

Just beyond Senhals, the track joins a village road (Moselweinstrasse), which bears L away from the river to reach the main road at a roundabout. Turn R on a cycle track beside the road. ▸ Continue following the river around a long R bend for 5km, passing **Briedern** opposite, to reach **Poltersdorf** (accommodation, refreshments, camping). The cycle track follows the road a little away from the river, passing a campsite R, then returns to the riverside by the Beilstein ferry ramp (26km, 88m) (camping, refreshments). The small village of **Beilstein** (pop. 160) (accommodation, refreshments, tourist office) lies on the opposite bank of the river.

Continue ahead at the roundabout and follow a road zigzagging up the hillside to reach Nehren Roman graves.

Beilstein is a popular location for film-makers

Much favoured by film and TV companies as a location for period dramas, **Beilstein** has maintained an almost unspoilt medieval appearance. The ruins of Metternich castle stand on the slopes above. The village can be visited by using the frequent cycle ferry across the Mosel.

Continue through **Ellenz** (accommodation, refreshments) to reach **Fankel** dam and locks, where a control room beside the dam regulates the flow of the river for its whole length through the gorge. Pass **Bruttig** opposite R then go under Bruttig bridge. At a distance of 200m after the bridge, zigzag R then L to drop down to the riverbank. Continue into **Ernst** (accommodation, refreshments), where the cycle track comes back close to the road. Pass a large monastery complex at **Ebernach** L.

Originally a Benedictine abbey that was dissolved during the Napoleonic invasion (1802), **Ebernach** is now a Franciscan foundation with a large institute to care for the intellectually disabled.

Continue, first past **Sehl**, and then past **Cochem castle** on the hilltop L. At the beginning of Cochem, bear R to follow the cycle track alongside the riverside, and continue past boat ramps then through gardens and a car park to reach **Cochem** bridge (36km, 85m, 50**Mkm**) (accommodation, refreshments, YH, camping, tourist office, cycle shop, station).

Cochem (pop. 5000) is the most popular tourist destination on the Mosel, with over 2.5 million visitors annually drawn by the well-preserved old town. The first castle was built on a hill above the town in about 1020. After several centuries of being passed between various local rulers, Cochem came under the control of the archbishop of Trier in 1294 and, except for a few short periods of French control, remained as such for 500 years.

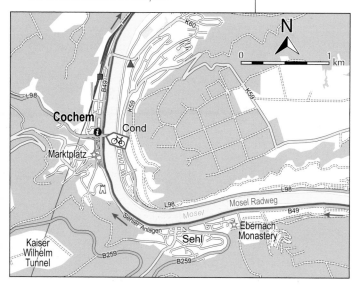

Cochem castle towers over Cochem

In the 14th century a heavy chain was used to block the river and collect tolls from passing traders, raising funds to expand the castle and fortify the town. The castle was blown up in 1689 during a period of French occupation and lay in ruins until it was bought in 1866 by Louis Ravené, a rich industrialist, who rebuilt it in a Gothic revival style as his summer residence. Nowadays it is open to the public.

STAGE 14
Cochem to Koblenz

Start	Cochem bridge (85m)
Finish	Koblenz, Deutsches Eck (62m)
Distance	51.5km
Waymarking	Mosel-Radweg

Beyond Cochem the gorge widens a little and meanders less. Vineyards, woods and castles still line the valley sides. The Mosel ends at Deutsches Eck in Koblenz, where it joins the Rhine to flow onwards to the North Sea. The route follows a mixture of asphalt cycle tracks, cycle lanes and quiet roads.

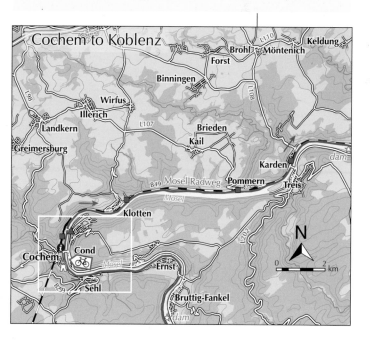

Karden Amtshaus, which dates from 1562

Continue north under **Cochem** bridge on a cycle track beside the river that proceeds through gardens and an extensive coach park for tour buses. The cycle track bears R and becomes red asphalt. It then passes under a road bridge and moves L to become a cycle lane on the main road, separated from the traffic by studs and double white lines. In **Klotten** (3.5km, 90m) (accommodation, refreshments, station), a separate cycle track reappears, running between parking spaces and the Mosel. Beyond the village, a cycle track alongside the road is followed for 5.5km, passing a sundial high up on the hillside L and a campsite R, to reach **Pommern** (9km, 84m) (accommodation, refreshments, camping, station).

After Pommern, the route becomes a cycle lane again. Drop down R on a separate cycle track under Treis-Karden bridge, with **Treis** across the river R, and continue along the riverside past **Karden** (11.5km, 83m) (accommodation, refreshments, camping, tourist office, cycle shop, station).

Treis-Karden (pop. 2250) are twin towns spread-eagling the Mosel. Karden (left bank) grew around an early Christian community founded by St Kastor, whose name lives on in the old monastery, school and parish church. The latter contains rediscovered medieval frescoes from 1495 and a Sturm organ of 1728. On the right bank, two ruined castles stand on the hillside overlooking Treis.

Continue along an on-road cycle lane right beside the river, passing Müden **dam** and locks R and **Müden** L (accommodation, refreshments, station) to reach **Moselkern** (17km, 79m) (accommodation, refreshments, camping, station), where there is a turn-off L to **Burg Eltz** castle. ▶

Continue below partly ruined **Burg Bischofstein** castle L (which houses a holiday centre for school children), mostly on a cycle lane but with a section of cycle track, past **Burgen** on the opposite bank of the river, to reach **Hatzenport** (22.5km, 77m) (accommodation, refreshments, camping, tourist office, station).

At the beginning of the village the cycle lane on the R of the road ends and you need to cross over and cycle through the village on the service road (Moselstrasse) L of the main road, past the Hatzenport ferry tower R. At the end of the village cross back to a cycle lane R of the road and follow the river around a bend L, passing **Brodenbach** across the river R, to reach **Löf** (accommodation, refreshments, station). In the village the cycle lane ends and it is again necessary to cross the road and cycle through the village along a service road L of the main road. Pass under a road bridge, cross the bridge approach road coming in from the L then immediately turn R across the main road back to the riverside. Follow the cycle lane, passing **Alken** on the opposite bank, with **Burg Thurant** castle towering above it, to reach **Kattenes** (27km, 78m) (accommodation, refreshments, station).

At the beginning of the village, the cycle lane switches to the L of the road, and stays on the L for 700m beyond the village before turning L under the railway.

Eltz castle is a fairy-tale castle of towers, turrets and gables, 5km uphill along the Eltztal valley. It cannot be seen from the cycle route.

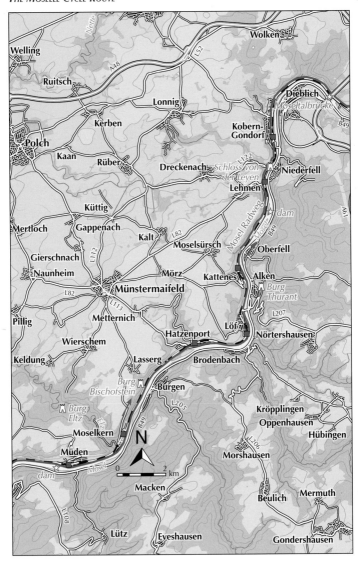

Turn R on a cycle track parallel to the railway and follow this into **Lehmen** (31km, 81m) (accommodation, refreshments, station).

The main road passes through Schloss von der Leyen

Emerge onto a road (Im Oberdorf) and continue, past a level crossing R, into Hauptstrasse. Bear R at a crossroads (still Hauptstrasse) and continue through the village. Where the road divides beyond the last buildings, fork L on the upper level. Follow the road bearing L (Münsterberg) and, after 100m, turn R (Römerstrasse). Continue ahead, zigzagging R then L past **Schloss von der Leyen** palace R, to run parallel to the railway.

> **Schloss von der Leyen** palace, the only waterside castle on the Mosel, was the home of the von der Leyen family, who provided a number of 18th-century prince–archbishops of Trier. Its most unusual aspect is that the riverside road and railway pass through the middle of the castle.

Soon after passing Schloss von der Leyen the track passes another castle, Schloss Liebieg L. Pass under a yellow road bridge and enter **Gondorf** (accommodation,

*Moseltalbrücke
soars 137m above
the Mosel near
Winningen*

refreshments, station). Continue on Bahnhofstrasse and follow this, with the railway R, into **Kobern** (34km, 74m) (accommodation, refreshments, tourist office).

Turn L at a crossroads and immediately R (Fährstrasse). Continue into Marktplatz, becoming Marktstrasse, through the attractive centre of Kobern, with old wineries and half-timbered houses. Keep ahead to leave the village on a quiet street with an artificial sports pitch L and railway R. Continue on a cycle track parallel with the railway – with vineyards rising steeply L – and follow this around a long bend R, passing under the **Moseltalbrücke** motorway bridge, which spans the whole gorge high above. Just before Winningen, follow the track as it bears L uphill through the vines to emerge onto Uhlenweg. This becomes vine-draped Marktstrasse, which leads to Marktplatz in the centre of **Winningen** (40km, 83m) (accommodation, refreshments, camping, tourist office, cycle shop, station).

In 1551, after a particularly bumper harvest, a wine festival was held in **Winningen** (pop. 2600), an ancient and extremely pretty wine town with many decorated houses and inns. The tradition continues every August and is Germany's longest running wine festival. After suffering badly during the Thirty Years' War, further calamity followed when the town became regarded as a centre of witchcraft, with 21 people sentenced to death for being witches or wizards between 1630 and 1661. The witches' fountain reflects these events.

The village was the birthplace of Augustus Horch (1868–1951), founder of the Audi car company. Horch initially worked in Mannheim for Karl Benz, maker of the first petrol-engine car, but he left in 1909 to establish his own company. He is buried in the cemetery. Just before Winningen, the graceful and delicate looking Moseltalbrücke motorway bridge, which passes 137m above the gorge, was the tallest bridge in Germany when opened in 1979. It has a main span of 218m.

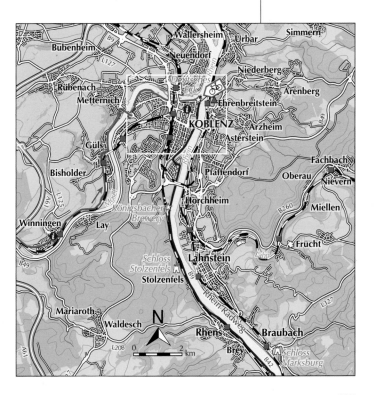

Turn R downhill (Bachstrasse) to reach an attractive square with frescoed and half-timbered buildings. Turn L, then cross a main road (L then R on a staggered cross-roads) into Bahnhofstrasse, continuing parallel with the railway. Just before the station, fork L (Röttgenweg) to pass the station at a slightly higher level. This becomes a quiet road, winding first through the vineyards of Winninger Brückstück then later past weekend cabins. After 3km this road reaches the first residential suburbs of Koblenz. Continue on Gülisastrasse past a station R and a church with two slender spires L. ◄ This leads to the centre of **Güls** (44.5km, 79m) (accommodation, refreshments, camping, station).

This street is designated as no entry for vehicles, but contra-flow traffic is permitted for cycles.

Reach a T-junction, where you zigzag R and immediately L (Planstrasse). Turn R after 100m (Stauseestrasse) and follow this street downhill to a T-junction beside the Mosel. Cross the riverside road (Moselweinstrasse) and turn L on a cycle track between the road and the river. Follow this as it becomes Winninger Strasse and

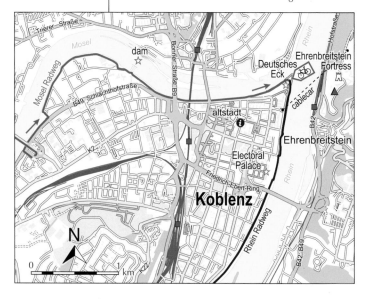

The final bridge over the Mosel in Koblenz

bears away from the river. Cross a side road that drops down to the river and, just before traffic lights, turn R on a cycle track beside the road to cross the Mosel on Kurt-Schumacher-Brücke.

Once over the river follow the cycle track, curving R, then fork L under the bridge approach road. Turn immediately R, then cross the riverside road ahead (Schlachthofstrasse) and turn R along a riverside cycle track. After passing under the bridge, follow the road away from the river past tennis courts and a small car park L. Turn L to go through a barrier at the end of the car park, and make your way between buildings back to the riverbank. Turn R on a riverside cycle track (Willy-Brandt-Ufer). Pass through a barrier and turn L at a T-junction (Pastor-Klein-Strasse). Pass Koblenz dam and locks L. ▶ Continue on Peter-Altmeier-Ufer, passing under three bridges. Follow the cycle track away from the road, beside the river, passing boat landing stages L, to reach the huge Kaiser-Wilhelm monument that stands at **Deutsches Eck**, the point where the Mosel joins the Rhine in **Koblenz** (51.5km, 62m, 0**Mkm**, 591**Rkm**) (accommodation, refreshments, YH, camping, tourist office, cycle shop, station).

There is a fish ladder to allow fish to migrate up the Mosel here.

KOBLENZ

Originally founded by the Romans in 8BC, Koblenz (pop. 106,000) gets its name from the Latin *confluentes* ('at the merging of rivers'). It was the seat of the archbishop and prince-elector of Trier from 1018 until 1794, when the French captured the Rhineland and deposed the archbishop. The Residenzschloss electoral palace was built in 1778–1786 as a residence for the archbishop. Fought over and occupied by the French on a number of occasions, the city became part of Prussia after the Congress of Vienna (1815). Between 1850 and 1858, the palace, as residence for the Prussian military governor of the Rhineland, was home to the crown prince and future emperor Wilhelm I and his wife Augusta, who became fond of the city. The Prussians heavily fortified Koblenz, centring on the great Ehrenbreitstein citadel that overlooks the city from the east bank of the Rhine. The citadel continued in use as a fortress until 1890 and it was the German military's headquarters during the First World War. During the Second World War, the *Altstadt* ('Old Town') near the confluence of Rhine and Mosel was mostly destroyed, but it was subsequently rebuilt to its original design. Always a military town, Koblenz is nowadays the headquarters of the German army forces command.

The city's most famous monument, a 14m-high bronze statue of Kaiser Wilhelm I (the world's largest equestrian statue), was erected at Deutsches Eck in 1897. This monument, a symbol of German unification after 1871, was placed in a location overlooking the junction of the Rhine and Mosel, to mark the incorporation of the former French Moselle territory into Germany. After destruction by US artillery in 1945, the pieces were kept and eventually recast, finally being reinstated to celebrate German re-unification in 1993. Around the plinth are the flags of all the German Länder (those for former East German states were added following the fall of the Berlin Wall). The riverside gardens between the palace and Deutsches Eck were landscaped and linked across the Rhine by cablecar to Ehrenbreitstein, as part of the German national gardening festival in 2011.

EXCURSION 2

Koblenz to St Goar: the Rhine Gorge

Start	Koblenz, Deutsches Eck (62m)
Finish	St Goar ferry (81m)
Distance	37km
Waymarking	Rhein-Radweg

What better way to finish your ride than a visit to the most scenic part of one of the world's greatest rivers? This excursion into the Rhine Gorge goes as far as St Goar and the famous Loreley Rock. There is spectacular scenery, as the Rhine forges its way between the Hunsrück and Taunus mountain ranges, accompanied by two roads, two railways and a cycle track. A series of pretty riverside towns are passed, including Boppard. The gorge sides are covered by vineyards and forest, with numerous romantic castles standing sentinel above. Most of the route is on good-quality cycle tracks along the riverside. Return is possible by train, boat or by cycling back along the other side of the river.

From Deutsches Eck in **Koblenz** follow the Rhine promenade south, passing a series of landing stages L. Continue through gardens (landscaped for the German national garden festival in 2011), with the Residenzschloss electoral palace R. Continue under Pfaffenderferbrücke bridge and pass Weindorf restaurant complex and a statue of Empress Kaiserin Augusta, both R. Dogleg L on a concrete block track through gardens and, just before an overbridge, turn L through a barrier uphill on an asphalt track. Bear L onto a road and cross a bridge over the marina into Mozartstrasse. Continue across a roundabout into Beethovenstrasse and turn R (Rheinau) along the Rhine flood dyke to leave Koblenz.

Continue through a barrier on a rough track, passing under railway and autobahn bridges, to reach a gravel track along the flood dyke under trees. Pass the

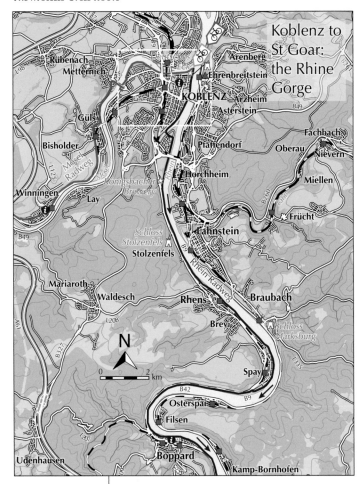

Koblenz to
St Goar:
the Rhine
Gorge

Königsbacher brewery R and continue along the riverbank on a gravel track below the railway. Pass **Lahnstein**
opposite and continue below **Schloss Stolzenfels** castle
R, the best-preserved of all Rhine castles. Turn R uphill
away from the riverbank, then turn L between houses

onto Brunnenstrasse, and continue past a beer garden on the riverbank. A bumpy section of cobbled road leads past Renser mineral water factory L, where a drinking fountain runs with naturally carbonated mineral water. A concrete block track continues through allotments. Pass a boat quay L, then bear L onto the riverbank. Pass Königstuhl hotel R and continue on Am Rhein past **Rhens** station (11km, 72m) (accommodation, refreshments, tourist office, station).

Pass between a campsite R and boat ramp L, with views of **Schloss Marksburg** castle above **Braubach** on the opposite side of the Rhine. Continue on a cycle track beside Holgertsweg and pass a large factory (Schottel) that produces rudder/propellers for boats. Bear L along the riverbank (Rheinufer) past **Spay** (15km, 69m) (accommodation, refreshments, station).

A marker stone in **Spay** indicates the halfway point along the navigable Rhine between Basle and Rotterdam (414km each way). There are many pretty red and white *fachwerkhäuser* (half-timbered

Marksburg castle

Brothers' castles,
Sterrenberg and
Liebenstein

buildings) including one with flood marks showing the highest flood three metres above the flood dyke (1882), and recent floods including 1993 and 1995, close to this level.

Follow Rheinufer as it bears slightly away from the river between meadows L and allotments R. Turn R away from the river and, after 100m, turn L beside Peter's chapel into Mainzer Strasse. Follow this ahead as it joins the main road, with Sonneck campsite on the riverbank L, and continue along a cycle track between road and river for 5km. Extensive vineyards cover the gorge sides R as the river makes a 180° bend L. Just as you reach the first house in Boppard, turn L between houses and immediately turn R along the riverbank. After 150m, dogleg R then L, continuing past a modern retirement home R. Beside the first boat pier, dogleg R then L onto Rheinallee, the promenade through **Boppard** (22.5km, 73m, 569**Rkm**) (accommodation, refreshments, camping, tourist office, cycle shop, station). ◀

To reach Marktplatz
in the centre of
the walled town of
Boppard, where there
are many attractive
half-timbered
houses, turn R into
Kronen-Gasse.

Continue on the promenade past ferry and gardens L. Pass under the clubhouse of a sports club and, where the road turns away from the river, continue ahead on a cycle path along the riverbank out of Boppard. Emerge beside the main road and continue on a cycle track between road and river past Sterrenberg and Liebenstein (**Brothers' castles**; see p196) opposite R to reach **Bad Salzig** (27km, 70m) (accommodation, refreshments, station).

Continue past **Hirzenach** and on under a road flyover past a marina at **Fellen**, with Maus castle visible across the river. Enter St Goar, passing another marina L, with Burg Rheinfels castle above R, and follow the main road (Rheinstrasse) as it bears L to bypass the old town centre. ▶ Bear L onto a cycle path through gardens beside the road. Continue through a car park and along a main road to reach the end of the stage at **St Goar ferry** (37km, 81m, 556**Rkm**) (accommodation, refreshments, YH, camping, tourist office, station).

To visit the old centre of St Goar, fork R (Heerstrasse) and continue along a pedestrianised street, which returns to the main road before the ferry.

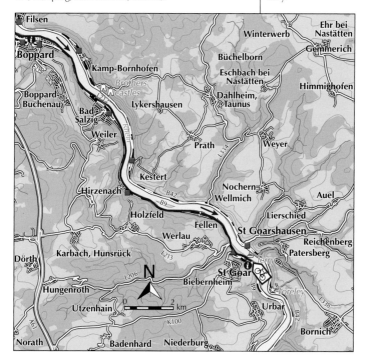

STERRENBERG AND LIEBENSTEIN

The two castles of Sterrenberg and Liebenstein are subjects of a legend of two brothers, sons of the lord of Sterrenberg, and their cousin Angela, who came to live with them when her father died. Both brothers were attracted to Angela. Henry, the restrained elder brother, kept his feelings secret, while his impetuous sibling Conrad wooed her and won her hand. Before they could marry the Crusaders passed by, recruiting volunteers to fight the Turks. Conrad went away to war, leaving Henry to look after his fiancée. Years passed and the old lord built a second castle, Liebenstein, across a narrow defile from Sterrenberg as a home for his younger son and niece when they married. Eventually, war was over and Conrad returned – accompanied by a Grecian princess he had married while away. Henry was furious and challenged his brother to a duel, but Angela came between them, urging them not to fight over her. She then went off to become a nun. Henry had a wall built between the castles so he should not see Conrad. After a cold winter in Germany, the princess fled south with a passing knight. Grief-stricken, Conrad threw himself from the battlements and died. Both castles still stand, with the high wall between them standing as testimony to this tragic tale.

Extension to Loreley Rock

To reach or view **Loreley Rock**, 2km beyond St Goar, you have three choices. You could continue on the west bank, passing a campsite below L to a viewpoint opposite the Loreley (accommodation, refreshments). Or you could cross the river by ferry to **St Goarshausen** and turn R, following the east bank to the base of the rock, where you can leave your cycle and walk up a steep path to the summit.

The recommended option, however, is to cross on the **ferry**, turn R along the riverbank and, after 250m, turn L onto Forstbachstrasse, which winds its way steeply for 3km to the top of the gorge, where a road R (signed Loreley) leads to the viewpoint on top of the rock (4km from St Goarshausen ferry; max altitude reached: 269m) (accommodation, refreshments).

Loreley Rock is a sheer promontory jutting out from the east bank of the Rhine, forcing the river to make

St Goar and Rheinfels castle

a sharp turn. The cliffs are 120m high, with a viewpoint and restaurant on top. Beneath the cliff, the river bend is partly obstructed by underwater rocks, leaving a narrow navigable channel with treacherous currents.

The legend of the Loreley tells of a fair maiden who, having been spurned by her fisherman boyfriend, swore vengeance upon all river-farers. She sat atop the cliff singing alluring songs to attract them towards the rocks and their doom. Nowadays, although the river has been dredged, these are still dangerous waters, and larger boats take on a pilot to navigate past the Loreley. A bronze statue of the siren, marked by a flag, sits at the end of a long narrow spit on the right bank, just downstream of the rock.

APPENDIX A
Route summary table

Stage	Start	Finish	Distance	Waymarking	Page
1	Col de Bussang, Moselle source (715m)	Remiremont, Rue des 5ème et 15ème BCP (388m)	36km	Voie Verte des Hautes Vosges (Bussang to Remiremont)	43
2	Remiremont, Rue des 5ème et 15ème BCP (388m)	Épinal, pedestrian bridge (326m)	28.5km	None (follow the D42)	53
3	Épinal, pedestrian bridge (326m)	Charmes, Place Henri Breton (284m)	28km	None, but route follows the Canal des Vosges throughout	60
4	Charmes, Place Henri Breton (284m)	Nancy, Rue Molitor (196m)	47.5km	None to Méréville, then Boucles de la Moselle to Nancy.	66
4A	Charmes, Place Henri Breton (284m)	Toul bridge (204m)	60.5km	None to Méréville, then Boucles de la Moselle to Toul	75
5A	Toul bridge (204m)	Pont-à-Mousson bridge (181m)	49.5km	Boucles de la Moselle (intermittent) to Frouard, then none	82
5	Nancy, Rue Molitor (196m)	Pont-à-Mousson bridge (181m)	35km	Boucles de la Moselle to Frouard, then none	89
6	Pont-à-Mousson bridge (181m)	Metz, Pont Éblé (164m)	33km	None to Novéant-sur-Moselle, then Véloroute Charles-le-Téméraire	96

Stage	Start	Finish	Distance	Waymarking	Page
7	Metz, Pont Éblé (164m)	Thionville bridge (153m)	30km	Véloroute Charles-le-Téméraire	107
8	Thionville bridge (153m)	Remich esplanade (142m)	39km	Chemin de la Moselle to Schengen, then PC3	114
9	Remich esplanade (142m)	Trier, Kaiser-Wilhelm-Brücke (130m)	43km	PC3 to Wasserbillig, then Mosel-Radweg	121
9A	Remich esplanade (142m)	Trier, Kaiser-Wilhelm-Brücke (130m)	85.5km	PC7, PC11, PC1, PC2, PC4	129
Exc 1	Konz, Mosel railway bridge (131m)	Merzig station (173m)	49.5km	Saar Radweg	142
10	Trier, Kaiser-Wilhelm-Brücke (130m)	Leiwen riverside (119m)	32.5km	Mosel-Radweg	151
11	Leiwen riverside (119m)	Bernkastel bridge (110m)	30km	Mosel-Radweg	157
12	Bernkastel bridge (110m)	Zell bridge (99m)	42km	Mosel-Radweg	165
13	Zell bridge (99m)	Cochem bridge (85m)	36km	Mosel-Radweg	173
14	Cochem bridge (85m)	Koblenz, Deutsches Eck (62m)	51.5km	Mosel-Radweg	181
Exc 2	Koblenz, Deutsches Eck (62m)	St Goar ferry (81m)	37km	Rhein-Radweg	191
		Total distance (main route)	512km		

APPENDIX B

Language glossary

English	French	German
barrier	*barrière*	*Sperre*
bicycle	*vélo*	*Fahrrad*
castle	*château*	*Schloss*
cathedral	*cathédrale*	*Dom*
church	*église*	*Kirche*
cycle track	*véloroute*	*Radweg*
cyclist	*cycliste*	*Radfahrer*
dam	*barrage*	*Damm*
diversion	*déviation*	*Umleitung*
dyke	*levée*	*Deich*
ferry	*bac*	*Fähre*
field	*champ*	*Feld*
floods	*inondation*	*hochwasser*
forest/woods	*forêt/bois*	*Wald/Walder*
fort	*fort*	*Festung*
lock	*écluse*	*Schleuse*
monastery	*monastière*	*Kloster*
monument	*monument*	*Denkmal*
motorway	*autoroute*	*Autobahn*
one way street	*sens unique*	*Einbahnstrasse*
puncture	*crevaison*	*Reifenpanne*
railway	*chemin de fer*	*(Eisen)bahn*
river	*fleuve*	*Fluss*
riverbank	*rive*	*Ufer*
road closed	*route fermée*	*Strasse gesperrt*
station	*gare*	*Bahnhof*
tourist information office	*syndicat d'initiative*	*Fremdenverkehrsbüro*
town hall	*hôtel de ville/mairie*	*Rathaus*
youth hostel	*auberge de jeunesse*	*Jugendherberge*

APPENDIX C
Useful contacts

Cycle Touring Club (CTC)
0844 736 8450
cycling@ctc.org.uk
www.ctc.org.uk

Youth Hostels Association
0800 0191700
customerservices@yha.org.uk
www.yha.org.uk

Hostelling International (YHA)
www.hihostels.com

Rail Europe (SNCF)
0844 848 4064
www.raileurope.co.uk

Deutsche Bahn (DB)
0871 8808066 (UK)
+49(0)180 5996633
www.bahn.com

P & O Ferries
08716 642121 (UK)
+44(0)1304 863000 (outside UK)
+31(0)20 200 8333 (NL)
www.poferries.com

Stena Line
0844 770 7070
www.stenaline.co.uk

Eurostar
0844 822 5822
www.eurostar.com

European Bike Express
01430 422111
info@bike-express.co.uk
www.bike-express.co.uk

The man in seat 61 (rail travel
information)
www.seat61.com

Stanfords
12–14 Long Acre
London WC2E 9LP
0207 836 1321
sales@stanfords.co.uk
www.stanfords.co.uk

The Map Shop
15 High St
Upton upon Severn,
Worcs WR8 0HJ
0800 085 40 80 or 01684 503146
themapshop@btinternet.com
www.themapshop.co.uk

Publicpress
www.publicpress.de

Bikeline Guides
www.esterbauer.com

Bett+Bike
www.bettundbike.de

Lorraine cycle routes
http://lorraine.voie.verte.free.fr

Luxembourg cycle routes
www.pch.public.lu

ADFC (German national cycling club)
www.adfc.de

Open Street Maps (online mapping)
www.openstreetmap.org

APPENDIX D

Principal tourist offices

Bussang
8 avenue de la Gare
88540
+33 (0)3 29 61 50 37
www.tourisme-bussang.com

St Maurice-sur-Moselle
28bis rue de Lorraine
88560
+33 (0)3 29 24 53 48
www.saint-maurice-vosges.com

Remiremont
4bis place de l'Abbaye
88205
+33 (0)3 29 62 23 70
www.ot-remiremont.fr

Épinal
6 place Saint-Goery
88008
+33 (0)3 29 82 53 32
www.tourisme-epinal.com

Charmes
19 rue Maurice Barres
88131
+33 (0)3 29 66 01 86
www.tourisme-charmes.fr

Nancy
Place Stanislas
54011
+33 (0)3 83 35 22 41
www.ot-nancy.fr

Toul
Parvis de la Cathédrale
54205
+33 (0)3 83 64 90 60
www.lepredenancy.fr

Liverdun
1 place d'Armes
54460
+33 (0)3 83 24 40 40
www.tourisme-liverdun.com

Pont-à-Mousson
52 place Duroc
54700
+33 (0)3 83 81 06 90
www.tourisme-pontamousson.fr

Metz
2 place d'Armes
57007
+33 (0)3 87 55 53 76
http://tourisme.metz.fr

Thionville
16 rue du Vieux College
57100
+33 (0)3 82 53 33 18
www.thionvilletourisme.fr

Sierck-les-Bains
3, place Jean de Morbach
57480
+33 (0)3 82 83 74 14
www.otsierck.com

Schengen
rue Robert Goebbels
L-5444
+352 26 66 56 11
www.schengen-tourist.lu

Remich
4 rue Enz
L-5533
+352 23 69 84 88
www.remich.lu

Luxembourg City
30 place Guillaume
L-2011
+352 22 28 09
www.lcto.lu

Ehnen
115 rue du Vin
L-5416
+352 26 74 78 74
www.region-moselle.lu

Grevenmacher
10 route du Vin
L-6794
+352 75 82 75
www.grevenmacher.lu

Wasserbillig
Moselstrasse 1
54308
+49 6501 602666
www.lux-trier.info

Konz
Granastrasse 2
254329
+49 6501 7790
www.konz.de

Saarburg
Graf-Siegfrid-Strasse
54439
+49 6581 995980
www.saar-obermosel.de

Mettlach
Freiherr-vom-Stein-Strasse 64
66693
+49 6865 91150
www.tourist-info.mettlach.de

Merzig
Poststrasse 12
66663
+49 6861 80440
www.merzig.de

Trier
An der Porta Nigra
54228
+49 651 978080
www.tourist-information-trier.de

Schweich
Bruckenstrasse 46
54338
+49 6502 93380
www.schweich.de

Longuich
Maximinstrasse 26
54340
+49 6502 1716
www.longuich.de

Mehring
Bachstrasse 47
54346
+49 6502 1413
www.mehring-mosel.de

Leiwen
Römerstrasse 1
54340
+49 6507 3100
www.leiwen.de

Neumagen
Hinterburg 8
54347
+49 6507 6555
www.neumagen-dhron.de

Bernkastel-Kues
Gestade 6
54470
+49 6531 4023
www.bernkastel.de

Zeltingen
Uferallee 13
54492
+49 6532 2404
www.zeltingen-rachtig.de

Traben-Trabach
Bahnstrasse 22
56841
+49 6541 83980
www.traben-trabach.de

Pünderich
Raiffeisenstrasse 3
56862
+49 6542 900021
www.puenderich.de

Zell
Balduinstrasse 44
56856
+49 6542 96220
www.zellerland.de

Cochem
Endertplatz
56812
+49 2671 60040
www.cochem.de

Winningen
August-Horch-Strasse 3
56333
+49 2606 2214
www.winningen.de

Koblenz
Jesuitenplatz 2
56068
+49 261 130920
www.touristik-koblenz.de

Boppard
Oberstrasse 118
56154
+49 6742 3888
www.boppard.de

St Goarhausen
Bahnhofstrasse 8
56346
+49 6771 9100
www.loreley-touristik.de

APPENDIX E
Youth hostels

France

Stage 4
Château de Rémicourt
149 rue de Vandoeuvre
54600
Villers-les-Nancy
+33 3 83 27 73 67

Stage 6
AJ Plage
1 allée de Metz Plage
57000
Metz
+33 3 87 30 44 02
(64+ beds)

Carrefour
6 rue Marchant
57000
Metz
+33 3 87 75 07 26
(60 beds)

Luxembourg

Stage 8
31 Waïstrooss
L-5440
Remerschen
+352 26 66 73 1
(148 beds)

Stage 9A
Pfaffenthal
2 rue du Fort Olisy
L-2261
Luxembourg City
+352 22 68 89 20
(240 beds)

Germany

Excursion 1
Bottelter Strasse 8
54439
Saarburg
+49 6581 2555
(103 beds)

Herbergstrasse 1
66693
Dreisbach
+49 6868 270
(124 beds)

Stages 9 and 9A
An der Jugendherberge 4
54292
Trier
+49 651 146620
(228 beds)

Stage 11
Jugendherbergstrasse 1
54470
Bernkastel-Kues
+49 6531 2395
(96 beds)

Stage 12
Hirtenpfad 6
56841
Traben-Trarbach
+49 6541 9278
(172 beds)

Stage 13
Klottener Strasse
956812
Cochem
+49 2671 8633
(146 beds)

Stage 14
Festung Ehrenbreitstein
56077
Koblenz
+49 261 972870
(195 beds)

Excursion 2
Bismarckweg
1756329
St Goar
+49 6741 388
(126 beds)

LISTING OF CICERONE GUIDES

For full information on all our
guides, books and eBooks,
visit our website: **www.
cicerone.co.uk**.

Walking – Trekking – Mountaineering – Climbing – Cycling

Over 40 years, Cicerone have built up an outstanding collection of 300 guides, inspiring all sorts of amazing adventures.

Every guide comes from extensive exploration and research by our expert authors, all with a passion for their subjects. They are frequently praised, endorsed and used by clubs, instructors and outdoor organisations.

All our titles can now be bought as **e-books** and many as iPad and Kindle files and we will continue to make all our guides available for these and many other devices.

Our website shows any **new information** we've received since a book was published. Please do let us know if you find anything has changed, so that we can pass on the latest details. On our **website** you'll also find some great ideas and lots of information, including sample chapters, contents lists, reviews, articles and a photo gallery.

It's easy to keep in touch with what's going on at Cicerone, by getting our monthly **free e-newsletter**, which is full of offers, competitions, up-to-date information and topical articles. You can subscribe on our home page and also follow us on **Facebook** and **Twitter**, as well as our **blog**.

Cicerone – the very best guides for exploring the world.

CICERONE

2 Police Square Milnthorpe Cumbria LA7 7PY
Tel: 015395 62069 info@cicerone.co.uk
www.cicerone.co.uk